Heal Thy Mind

The Rhyme of Healing: The Octave's Method

O is for Observation, through stillness we find,
Meditation and breath work that quiet the mind.
In silence we listen, the answers are clear,
Awareness emerges, dissolving the fear.

C is for Compassion, for self and for all,
Embracing the good, the struggles, the fall.
With kindness we grow, we nurture, we mend,
Learning to love ourselves as we extend.

T is for Therapy, a path we explore,
Daily we practice, unlocking the door.
From journaling to mindfulness, healing begins,
Each step is a victory as peace settles in.

A is for Animals, and laughter so bright,
Like children at play, their joy taking flight.
With playfulness and movement, we rediscover the way,
To heal through the fun that we often delay.

V is for Victuals, nourishing and pure,
Detoxifying the body, keeping us sure.
We choose what we eat with intention and grace,
Fueling our journey, at our own pace.

E is for Exercise, where movement is free,
We stretch and we bend, in sweet harmony.
Flexibility grows, with choices we make,
In strength and in stillness, our bodies awake.

S is for Socialize, where self-growth begins,
Others reflect our triggers and the places within.
Through relationships, our true selves we find,
Growing and healing, with each tie that binds.

The OCTAVES Method, where all behavior makes sense,
We just need to find the sense it presents.
We just need to find the sense it presents.
We just need to find the sense it presents.

Heal Thy Mind

7 STRATEGIES TOWARD MENTAL
WELLNESS, HAPPINESS, AND SUCCESS

TONYA OCTAVE,
LICENSED CLINICAL SOCIAL WORKER (LCSW)

Tonya Octave, LCSW, Prof Corp;
DBA Multicultural Services, Prof Corp
California & Nevada

https://www.tonyaoctave-lcsw.com/

Cover Design and Pictures: Tonya Octave, Prof Corp
Copyright @ 2022 Tonya Octave. All rights reserved.
ISBN: 979-8-4245-7690-4

Printed in the United States

First edition March 2022

All rights reserved. No portion of this book may be reproduced in any form without the permission from the publisher, except as permitted by the U.S. Copyright law. For permissions contact: info@tonyaoctave-lcsw.com

CONTENTS

DISCLAIMER 7

AUDIENCE 9

DEDICATION 11

MY PERSONAL JOURNEY TO MENTAL
WELLNESS, HAPPINESS, AND SUCCESS 13

1. OBSERVATION: SPIRITUAL HEALTH 17

2. COMPASSION: EGO HEALTH 37

3. THERAPY: EMOTIONAL AND
   MENTAL HEALTH 55

4. ANIMALS: PLAYFUL INNER HEALTH 77

5. VICTUALS: NUTRITION HEALTH 101

6. EXERCISE: PHYSICAL HEALTH 121

7. SOCIALIZE: RELATIONSHIP HEALTH 131

NEXT STEPS: A GUIDE TO
A HEALTHY LIFE 141

CITATIONS 151

RECOMMENDED RESOURCES 159

DISCLAIMER

This book is for informational purposes only and is not intended to diagnose, treat, cure, or prevent any illness or disease. The material for this book is also not intended as a substitute for seeking out professional assistance. The information contained in this book is simply to give you some direction of where to start and how to keep going so you are moving towards wellness. This book does not indicate a patient/practitioner relationship. However, if you want to seek professional help, you can email me at info@tonyaoctave-lcsw.com or visit my website https://tonyaoctave-lcsw.com/ for questions about your journey towards mental wellness. It is advised that you consult your physician, attorney, and integrative and functional health professionals regarding the suggestions and ideas noted in this book. Using this book and its information implies that you understand and accept this disclaimer.

AUDIENCE

This book aims to help everyday people who want suggestions and ideas about improving their overall health, including early career professionals, college students, young parents, elderly adults, and relatively active individuals. You are encouraged to buy this book for yourself and those on their wellness journey. This book is a collection of my ideas gathered over the last twenty-plus years of experience. Therefore, I make no guarantees regarding your success in implementing these strategies. Accepting the risk involved, you understand that the steps towards wellness are specific to each person, and what works for one person may or may not work for another. This book is just a starting point to begin your wellness journey.

DEDICATION

This text is dedicated to the Creator. I hope I live the life that pleases and serves you with compassion and humility. I appreciate all the life learning experiences provided to me; even though it was painful, it was necessary for my growth. I know my choices and decisions will continue to be guided through spirit and wisdom.

Thank you to my mom, Mary, and dad, Albert. I was born to you for several reasons, which continue to be discovered. Your lessons continue to teach me and guide me towards my purpose. You remained supportive and believed in me even when I was lost. Thank you for being available to me in your way.

To the two faithful, honest, and loyal men in my life. My lovely husband, Mike, you agreed to be on this journey with me many years ago. Our journey has had beautiful experiences, and you continue to live up to your word. You keep me grounded. I am honored to continue to share this journey with you.

To my brother Ed, you push and challenge me. Your intellectual strength is inspiring, and this teaches me to think deeply for myself. You listen to me in ways no one else can.

I am grateful to be blessed with the opportunity to take

part in the parenting of three children, Kamaoo Jr., Jasmine, and Justin. You inspire me to be a better mother, a better stepmom, a better woman, and a better human.

Lastly, to all the families, parents, children, social workers, psychologists, and integrative experts I met along the way, our work continues to inspire me, even though we may have spent limited time together. It is never limited but constantly occurring in my thoughts and actions. Interacting with you has inspired me to find and write practical solutions to the challenges we all face. You have been my teacher, and your willingness to do the challenging work is what made the material in this book possible. Thank you for the countless number of conversations, your desire to ask for help, the ability to influence your life, and for advocating for resources to make real change.

We all can "heal thy mind."

MY PERSONAL JOURNEY TO MENTAL WELLNESS, HAPPINESS, AND SUCCESS

I am a private practice clinician who helps people who have experienced trauma attain physical, mental, and spiritual wellness. Using an integrative approach based on an acronym of my last name, OCTAVES, I provide tools and guidance so that my patients can move towards healthy living, a positive mindset, and confidence. However, I am not just a clinician who guides and gives strategies. I have struggled with depression and anxiety, battled weight gain and the disease of Hashimoto's, and worked through identity issues. I am a bi-ethnic female raised by a single parent. In the early years, I knew and was loved by my daddy. When he suddenly became absent from my life in sixth grade, I felt abandoned.

Growing up poor, I struggled in school academically and had obstacles and setbacks because of my ethnicities and gender. In college, I got pregnant and had a child at twenty years old. My son's father and I stayed together for a time. Because of the increasing conflict that we both exhibited, we separated, and I became a single parent. However, I remained in school, worked two to three jobs, and was a single parent with no financial support.

All these events impacted my physical and emotional health. I experienced traumas through the stories of others without realizing it, and as this pattern continued, I became emotionally, spiritually, and physically unhealthy. I started to have health concerns, including obesity, precancerous thyroid, Hashimoto's disease, and hypoglycemia. I knew if I did not find another way, I was moving along a path of disease. So, I changed my life—physically, emotionally, and spiritually. Now, after many years of working on it, I am free from disease. My mental health is optimal, as I don't suffer, enabling me to assist others on their own wellness paths. Over a lifetime and after implementing the strategies explored in this book, I laugh easily and can find joy in everyday life. Eating healthy foods as a vegan, I also exercise and practice meditation, working to become the best I can be with a healthy mindset so that I can guide others. Building a positive rapport with my patients, I am skilled at helping others discover who they are, as well. If you are looking for strategies to improve your health and need hope to heal and move toward wellness, this book will be a great tool to educate and assist you on your journey.

We will explore seven principles/strategies, one in each chapter, with the OCTAVES integrative method. In addition, there are reflection questions at the end of each chapter. I encourage you to use these questions as prompts to reflect on developing your mental health wellness plan. You can use one question per week or one question for several weeks.

1. Observation: Spiritual Health
2. Compassion: Ego Health
3. Therapy: Emotional and Mental Health
4. Animals: Playful Inner Health
5. Victuals: Nutrition Health
6. Exercise: Physical Health
7. Socialize: Relationship Health

1

OBSERVATION: SPIRITUAL HEALTH

Proverb: (Wo)man is to become God-like through a life of virtue and the cultivation of the spirit through scientific knowledge, practice, and bodily discipline. (Ancient African proverb)

Affirmation: I am grounded in this moment.

I became spiritually minded when I was in college at the University of California, Irvine, pursuing a degree in psychology cognitive science. Searching for meaning, I studied many different religions, including Islam, Christianity, Hinduism, and ancient Egyptian (Kemet) philosophy. I connected most with Kemet from ancient Egyptian civilization. It promotes the seven principles of MAAT: truth, justice, righteousness, propriety, balance, order, and harmony.

Now I routinely use these virtues in the way I think, the way I act, and the way I am. Practicing awareness and observing your spiritual health is one step of many towards obtaining wellness.

It can include practicing meditation and mindfulness, developing spiritual practices, building character in relationships, and promoting gratefulness.

Meditation

Psychological growth is accomplished because the mind is controlled. The thoughts are controlled, the intellect is strong, and internal harmony is the outcome. It needs to be consistent and persistent with practice. There are two forms of meditation. They are known as informal and formal approaches. Here are some methods of meditation I use with my patients.

Guided meditation: Using my voice and based on your

underlying needs, I will guide you to a place where you will achieve a deeply relaxed, calm, and meditative state. I may use images and visualizations to bring you towards peacefulness. This allows your mind to organize and imagine a place and reference point. It helps to control the thoughts and keep the mind active so that it does not wander. When there are many traumas, agitations in the mind, or uncontrolled or racing thoughts, imagery can add structure to the mind to support this calming state. It is a good beginner practice and can be beneficial if done with a trained professional.

Guided meditation includes using the five senses. Focusing on sight, taste, touch, smell, and hearing helps to change one's perceptions. Connecting with your senses and using visualization, you can implement healthy thinking.

Benefits of guided meditation:

1. You can focus your thinking.
2. You can develop a mental practice to train the mind.
3. It is specific, and goal directed. It provides structure.
4. It combines past perceptions with current perceptions, giving you control to make decisions.
5. It minimizes negative thought patterns. This is judgment-free.
6. You feel inspired and motivated to make a change, because your perception makes it possible.
7. It releases tensions that build up in the muscles.

Progressive muscle relaxation

In addition to using guided meditation, I implement progressive muscle relaxation. Using my voice as a guide, I direct you to focus on various parts of the body in turn. This involves the contracting and releasing of various muscles. It is best done in collaboration with psychotherapy. Progressive muscle relaxation can help make connections within the body, causing a reduction in symptoms and a relaxed state within the mind. When focused on one part of the body, you become aware of various sensations arising in the mind and body. In addition, you become more aware of the physical sensations in the body. With adults, I start from the toes up through the legs. With kids, it depends on their age.

Implementing muscle relaxation has multiple benefits.

It can decrease one's heart rate, reduce cortisol (stress hormone) in the body, lower blood pressure and respiration rate, decrease oxygen (giving the lungs a break), reduce muscle tension and chronic pain, improve sleep and digestion, lower fatigue (making you feel energized), and boost confidence. In addition, it reduces anger and aggression, decreasing symptoms of anxiety, depression, and irritability.

This relaxation practice works well with kids and adults. With kids, we play games such as "Can you make a tight fist, hold it, and then release?" and "Can you suck in your stomach as tight as you can, then release?" This is done with other body parts throughout a treatment session. For children and teens, competition is a form of motivation and encouragement. Practice usually lasts ten to fifteen minutes and is done two to three times during a session. The approach is less competitive for adults and usually lasts fifteen to thirty minutes.

Mindfulness

Besides guided meditation and muscle relaxation, mindfulness is another form of meditation. This technique is a way of practicing being present in the moment. It brings awareness to one's thoughts, feelings, and physical sensations through a loving and gentle mind. There is no "right" or "wrong." It is about awareness. Mindfulness is a form of meditation and a way of practicing being present in the moment, not worrying about the past (depression) or the future (anxiety). It is essential to control the mind and thoughts to achieve mental wellness. We often spend a lot of time in our thoughts. Our thoughts are like dreams that can trick us. Most of the time, the ego is activated. The desires and wishes of the person are influencing this process. I recall a time when I struggled with feelings of jealousy, especially in a romantic relationship. When I was alone because my partner was gone, I could get caught up in my thinking. This would easily convince me that he was cheating. He may have been cheating, but the process going on in my mind was disturbed. One thought would lead to another and another. It goes something like this.

"Why do I have to stay home all the time? It's not fair."

The idea of fairness can occupy my thoughts and convince me of so much. I am thinking, "He is probably not even at work. He probably met some girl..." Our thoughts tend to occupy the more negative path for many reasons, including the following:

1. Negativity is observed during childhood. Think about the adults in your life growing up. Did they complain a lot? Were they unhappy? Did they verbalize a negativistic point of view? An example: While driving in the car, a parent may say, "That person does not know how to drive." The focus of the problem is on

the other person. A series of events influence the child, and negative thinking patterns develop.

2. Negative thoughts develop from a loss of something. A loss is where you experience an underlying emotion of insecurity or abandonment. The fear associated with a loss activates your ego: the ego must protect itself, and in turn will look at the other person as the problem.

    For example, if I struggle with being insecure in a relationship, I may blame myself. I think, "I am not good enough for you." Through my behavior, I may push you away. I will experience the relationship as unsatisfying and believe I am to blame. The ego will put up defense mechanisms to protect you from this pain. You are thinking, "I can't lose another relationship, because then I will experience abandonment again." This is painful for the mind to accept, so a negative thought pattern will continue as protection.

3. There is a lack of balance within the mind-body-spirit connection, leading to distress and depressive symptoms. The disruption to this balance activates one's flight-fight or freeze responses.

4. One may not be caring for their instinctual needs. Lack of sleep, lack of proper nutrition, lack of pleasure in meaningful activities (reading, writing, being creative, being playful), and lack of exercise

(causing excess energy to build up in the body) can all lead to distressed health and negative thoughts.
5. Dissatisfaction with oneself in relationships with others, leading to interpersonal relationship challenges. One continues to think that the problem resides with other people, even when one believes they are working on themselves.

There are other reasons why we tend to drift towards negative ways of thinking. To implement wellness, we need to retrain our thinking processes. To deal with negative thoughts, you will need specialized training. A trained professional can help you identify your problem and resolve it.

Here is an example of how I can retrain my thoughts.
Initial thought: "I hate my relationship."

Retraining means making a new thought pattern.

"Although there are struggles in my relationship, they are my struggles, and I am learning more about me in this relationship. I can be kind to myself and understand the other person if they have a hard day. I can be calm instead of reacting with anger."

Another example is a police officer who needs to retrain their thoughts.

Initial thought: "I am afraid to go out, as many law-enforcement officers have gotten hurt or killed in the current climate. Many people are against us."

Retraining the thoughts: "Some officers have indeed been killed in the line of duty. But I like my job of protecting and helping others. I can go out, confident that I can do my best work. Some people respect us as officers of the law."

Besides retraining thoughts, I also encourage my patients to explore other forms of meditation, including mantras and breathwork, mind-body-spirit connections, and trauma-sensitive meditation.

Mantras: Supporting a deeper inner spiritual need, mantras go beyond the ego and towards a spiritual belief and connection. Sound and natural vibrations are used to support this deeper meditative state.

Breathwork: Breathing is vital to survival, bringing oxygen into the bloodstream and removing carbon dioxide. A complete cycle involves your diaphragm, stomach, spine, and mind. Research tells us that breathwork can support treatment associated with all types of traumas. It allows you to exhale carbon dioxide from your body, causing the blood to become more alkaline and retain more oxygen. This method can include chest breathing, diaphragmatic breathing, abdominal breathing, and clavicular breathing. Focused breathing connects the conscious and the subconscious minds. It is a mind-body-spirit connection.

Mind, body, and spirit connection

The mind encompasses the mental aspects, including the conscious mind, the subconscious, the unconscious, awareness, and fantasies. Primarily unseen, the mind focuses on thoughts, emotions, interpersonal interactions, and personality structures and formulations. The body encompasses the physical parts of the body—what you see internally and externally. My hair, my arms, and my legs, along with my organs and cells, are exchanges occurring within the body to keep this vessel working effectively. The soul/spirit is the essence of who we are. We have a deeper connection to the universe. It is beyond the physical and goes into deeper aspects of the world.

There is a saying that our soul is meant for heaven, and our body is intended for the earth. The two are interconnected. We are spirit. It is the primary source of our existence. The spirit has a human experience on earth through our bodies. The way I think of it, my body is just my clothing. It is tangible, something you can see, touch, feel, hear, and smell. However, it is just clothing to my spirit. Therefore, one can engage in acts that are pleasing to the spirit or to the body. If one chooses the body's pleasures, one can be led down a path to illness and disease. If one chooses to engage in acts pleasing to the spirit, one will be directed to happiness, bliss, and joy.

Trauma Sensitive Meditation

Beyond connecting the mind, body, and spirit, I use trauma-sensitive meditation. This method offers a space to give you opportunities and suggestions about your meditation practices, where you are free from judgment and ridicule of yourself. You will begin to explore different choices and options. For those with trauma history, their choice was taken away.

Trauma patients did not have a say in the trauma, especially with developmental trauma, which occurs in childhood during developmental stages, and complex trauma, which occurs in childhood and involves more than one form of abuse/neglect/maltreatment over months to years. Trauma takes away one's ability to think independently, resulting in many people who have linear and rigid ways of thinking and reacting. Trauma-sensitive meditation practice gives those people freedom of choice to make decisions, and sometimes that decision may be not to decide. Trauma-sensitive meditation works for many reasons.

1. We work on being present where the patient is at in the moment.
2. It creates a safe space.
3. There are no rules or judgments—just suggestions.

Other forms of meditation can be triggering and challenging, so continual practice is hard. One may struggle with silence, uncontrolled and negative thoughts, and trauma reminders. Using these meditations, one can work through the traumatic experiences and work towards wellness. Through trauma-sensitive meditation, patients can receive many benefits.

1. Patients work to understand, control, and change thinking patterns about abuse, both unconscious and conscious.
2. They are provided with choices, which is empowering and freeing.
3. They can participate in any way that is meaningful for them.
4. The trained clinician can help patients identify body-related triggers and emotions.
5. It provides an option for others about voice-choice-repair.

There are selective words used in trauma-sensitive meditation. I avoid giving directions. Instead of saying "we must" and "we should," I use the word "your" with my patients. This is your practice, your thinking, your exploration. It connects you to an internal experience. There is a shared meditative experience and energy exchange. We may experience a different practice. We may make different choices about this practice. Although trained and certified to do trauma-sensitive meditation, I move away from being a meditation expert. We are not engaging in a therapist-patient relationship, but I am a facilitator in our practice. We are both participants working collectively during this meditative experience. I use neutral language: "I welcome you to join in any way that suits you in this moment. You may choose to find a relaxing form for your body, knowing you can make many changes at any moment. You might simply take a breath. You may gently relax your body or simply tense your body, or you may just have little or no movements." (1)

Spiritualism/Religion

Meditative practices, combined with practicing spiritualism and religion, can enhance your wellness. Spiritualism and religion are socio-cultural systems that support society, providing a set of practices, morals, beliefs, and worldview perceptions. There are many practices worldwide, including ancient Egyptian and Indian beliefs, Hinduism, Buddhism, Taoism, Islam, Catholicism, Christianity, and hundreds more. Regardless of your thoughts, the common theme is God, a higher entity. To attain mental balance, one must choose a spiritual path that promotes mental peace, mental calmness, and mental discipline.

Besides finding peace through meditation and religious practices, you can build wellness by building trust, humility, compassion, and gratefulness and by loving yourself and others unconditionally.

Trust is the first emotion to develop in infancy. Is my parent trustworthy? Will they know my different cries, feed me, change my diaper? Can they meet my needs? Trust is more than faith. Trust represents being "special" enough for my parent(s) to meet my needs. Will I be given what I need to face life challenges? It is about letting go of fear, paranoia, and suspiciousness and at the same time acknowledging one's vulnerability. Trust is built over a lifetime, based on one's intuitive processes if we are mindful of our distortions. We all have many distortions. Trust is based on a deeper form of wisdom. Life is purposeful and meaningful. Trust is letting go of things—sometimes old thinking patterns, sometimes relationships, sometimes ideas and perceptions about you and others. It means believing others can be helpful and accepting help while acknowledging your vulnerability. All people are not all good all the time. Being aware of what is happening, you go through life with your eyes open, seeking the truth in yourself, in others, and in the world.

As a child, I was protected. My mother is Caucasian, and my father was African American. I have a brother who was older and protective and my closest and safest peer relationship. My mother encouraged and affirmed me, enabling me to trust others. She would tell me I was smart. It was more important than being pretty. As a single parent working multiple jobs, she still took time to do fun stuff, like reading to me or taking me to the zoo. I experienced the quality of this relationship, not the quantity, which was the amount of time spent together. Though it wasn't as accepted to have mixed children when I was young, she made sure to celebrate our Blackness. For example, she made sure that my hair was combed in the 1970s and 1980s styles to fit in with peers. Leaving a legacy, she wanted us, both my brother and me, to have a sense of being loved and secure.

Humility is the state of being modest and humble, of doing, feeling, and being good in the deepest part of who you are in this universe. This is expressed from the heart and not the ego. The ego can make you feel humble just to satisfy the ego. Still, genuine humbleness is a realization that everyone and everything is equally important, that no one is better than any other. With humility, you can listen openly, accepting that you may not discover all the answers. You are not there to solve problems for others. You have faith, trust, and belief in yourself. You have boundaries and limitations, bringing awareness and not allowing others to humiliate you, put you down, reject or destroy you, or make you feel less than you are. You are not beating yourself up, putting yourself down, or making yourself feel bad. All things are interconnected. If you criticize, reject, or judge others, you also criticize, reject, and judge yourself.

Compassion is a nonjudgmental awareness of how one understands themselves, others, and the interactions between the two. There is a selfless acceptance of who you are and of who other people are. There is an understanding that people act and react in ways based on their survival abilities, knowledge base, and psychological/emotional limitations. Working to destroy the ego and ideas about self-importance and pride, you must see the truth in oneself and others and take care of yourself and others in a loving way.

Gratitude is being thankful without the need or desire to repay or feel obligated. It removes judgement, worries, and doubts. You move towards enjoyment and happiness. Your heart is open, expressing thankfulness because you are receiving more than you desire. This is less about material stuff and more about the gifts of love. Others will be drawn to you, and your energy can influence them. Be grateful for things we take for granted, such as food, water, air, our bodies, our lungs, our ability to increase our knowledge, reading, math, science, walking, running—even the ability not to walk or run. It brings awareness that there is good in all things and an appreciation for self, others, and nature.

Loving unconditionally is acknowledging and accepting all parts of yourself and others, the good and the bad. This is a joyful state of appreciation and admiration, even interconnectedness with self, others, and nature. We are all interconnected to each other and to nature. You let go, allowing control to leave. It brings one into harmony, transforming anger into peace, fear into trust, insecurity into security. Loving unconditionally provides a good foundation for compassion, which will be discussed in Chapter 2: Compassion: Ego Health.

Takeaways

There are many ways to consider observation, from informal to formalized and ritualized mediations. What works for one may not work for others. So, try a variety of meditations. Don't give up because it is a new process. Sometimes people get discouraged. Someone told me if you can't meditate, then meditate more, not less. It's a practice. Retraining the mind from negative to positive takes time and patience. Work on patience. Some people are discouraged by religion. Go out there and explore; find the one that works for you. Explore your religion/spiritualism and be open and receptive to learning. Find a path that suits you, even if initially you feel alone and separated from friends and family. This is part of discovering yourself, your path, your truer authentic self.

HEAL THY MIND

Self-reflections

1. Who am I?
2. Where am I going?
3. What do I want?
4. What is my purpose?
5. Where do I come from?
6. Why am I here?
7. What am I grateful for?

2

COMPASSION: EGO HEALTH

Proverb: Every human being is the author of his/her own health or disease. (Buddhist proverb based on Ayurvedic healing)

Affirmation: I am likable; I am loveable; I am good enough.

When I was a little girl, I adored my daddy, and he loved me. He spoiled me, treating me like a princess. My parents were not living together, and I would visit him. I was Daddy's little girl, and he would give me anything I wanted. I felt loved and wanted. Over the years, he sometimes would help financially, but this was not consistent.

My mom encouraged our relationship. Being a single parent was financially a challenge for her. When I was in sixth grade, my mom requested child support, and eventually, the case went to court. After the court case, my dad dropped out of my life. Suddenly, there was no contact at all. Our relationship changed. I went from Daddy's little girl, spoiled and adored, to not seeing him. I felt abandoned and unloved. I felt a lot of anger. As I moved into my teenage years and adulthood, those feelings of abandonment translated into other relationships, especially with men. I struggled, going into a deep depression. In my twenties, while I was at the University of California, Irvine, I tried to reconnect with him and rebuild the relationship. It took more than twenty years for us to reconcile and for me to work through my stuff. I needed to forgive and let go while dealing with feelings of being unlovable and abandoned. Through my own experiences, I have learned to have compassion, to find healing in my life.

Compassion is the ability to be loving and accepting of yourself, all the good and the bad. To respect other people's perspectives while practicing self-care, forgiving people for wrongs committed against you, and making efforts to show kindness. To have compassion, you must first deal with your ego.

The ego

The ego can be thought of as an observer in your life. It is embedded within the personality structures. It shapes our personality. The desires of the Id (basic animalistic desires) and the superego (Wonder Woman and Superman complex) need balance. So, the ego is to provide this balance. The ego has a beautiful tendency to jump when there is resistance and defend itself against this resistance. These are defense mechanisms (fantasy, rationalization, projection, repression, suppression, reaction formation, regression, compensation, displacement, isolation of affect, sympathize, undoing, introjection, intellectualization, sublimation, and acting out are a few). Therefore, the ego needs attention and training, and once there is mastery, the ego needs to be destroyed. Typically, most will not destroy the ego without being grounded in a "true" authentic spiritual/religious practice. However, you can develop mentally, physically, and spiritually to balance the ego. One way is through self-care. Self-care has many aspects, including supporting your physical, personal, and intellectual needs, improving your social expression and communication, and investing in yourself financially and in your work life. It also means doing more profound reflection, forgiving others, and showing kindness.

Self-care

It is essential to take care of your physical needs, including getting enough sleep and exercise, decreasing environmental toxins and pesticides, and making sure you have quality drinking water and are eating organic foods. Experts at the Centers for Disease Control and Prevention recommend that each age group have the following amount of sleep per day:

- Newborns (0–3 months): 14–17 hours
- Infants (4–12 months): 12–16 hours, including naps
- Toddler (1–2 years): 11–14 hours, including naps
- Preschool (3–5 years): 10–13 hours, including naps
- School-age (6–12 years): 9–12 hours
- Teenagers (13–18 years): 8–10 hours
- Adults: 7–9 hours, depending on the age (3).

Quality sleep is not so much about the length of time as it is about feeling rested when you wake up. Ideally, you should be able to drift off to sleep in about 30 minutes. However, if you are tossing and turning or frequently waking up in the middle of the night, or if you wake up feeling tired, you may not be getting quality sleep. Consuming alcohol or coffee can be a big issue affecting sleep quality. Lack of sleep can contribute to health problems, including a weak immune system, heart disease, forgetfulness, weight gain, depression, and anxiety, and seasonal affective disorder. In my sessions, I ask my patients about the quantity and quality of their sleep. If you don't have a "good" quality sleep and it affects your productivity, you can create a plan to improve your sleeping habits.

Here are some suggestions and tools to improve sleep:

1. No alcohol or coffee within four to six hours of going to bed.
2. Drink lavender or chamomile tea.
3. Take melatonin.
4. Meditate by sitting in silence or listening to something calming.
5. Journal either on paper or video, as it helps release anxiety.
6. Eat protein such as peas, spinach, kale, broccoli, or sprouts before bed.
7. Turn off your phone and put it in another room.
8. Keep your room cool and dark.
9. Create a consistent routine around going to bed. (2 & 6)

Besides getting adequate sleep, two things that can improve health are practicing good hygiene and getting massages (bodywork). To see the overall picture and work toward wellness, I discuss environmental issues with clients, including safety, stability, and healthy habits. Encouraging them to decrease toxins, chemicals, and pesticides while addressing poor-quality water and food choices are helpful.

Improving personal health

After addressing physical and environmental needs, I encourage clients to look at ways to strengthen their health, including boosting cognitive functioning, improving communication and social interaction, and investing in themselves. For example, if you read, write, or do math, you stimulate brain functioning. Likewise, if you learn a new skill, you enhance creativity and problem-solving abilities.

It is essential to practice active listening and develop compassion to improve social interaction skills. Active listening means paying attention to what the other person is saying and the deeper meaning of the interaction. You must be intentional in building active listening skills.

Limiting distractions while conversing, such as turning off your phone or TV and reflecting on what you have learned, is helpful. In addition, if you ask clarifying questions, you can better understand the other person's point of view.

Developing compassion begins by expressing thoughts that are not judgmental or accusing. Releasing control, you can be honest, compassionate, and loving. Without making assumptions, you can provide space to acknowledge the behavior. Avoid accusing or belittling language. It is vital to practice trust in relationships. I tell people to slow down and quiet the mind and the body. Silence gives you so much. It is a blessing. When you are silent, you can reflect. It allows you to release control. The process of slowing down with no pressure enables you to figure out ways to respond compassionately and lovingly.

While building effective listening skills, you can also improve perspective by investing in yourself financially, using money to gain more education, training, and knowledge. If you enjoy your job, you most likely will be satisfied with your work productivity. Happiness in work can improve your relationships, increase your motivation to progress, boost your self-worth, and stimulate your intellect. Early in my career, I worked for child protective services. I saw so much pain in the foster care system. It was horrible. If you were poor, you were treated differently. I experienced direct and indirect acts of racism as well as institutional bias. I worked for over ten years in different departments, fighting social injustice and developing programs to address human trafficking, battling racial disproportionality. With a master's degree and all my experience, I applied for a higher management job in the system but didn't get it. I believe it was because of institutional bias and racism. This happened a few times during this career. It was frustrating. I didn't realize how much stress and trauma I was managing until after leaving.

Now that I am a private practice clinician, helping people discover health and wellness, I have less stress and anxiety. Satisfied with my work, I am joyful at the end of the day and can sleep well at night. So, you see, some things happen in our lives, and we make choices to continue the suffering, or we make choices to change.

Deeper work

Developing self-care with an emphasis on physical, personal, and intellectual aspects is one of many ways to improve wellness. Another method is implementing deeper inner work.

Deeper inner work deals with defenses, controlling negative self-talk, learning forgiveness, identifying triggers and ways to work through triggers, and practicing compassion and kindness.

Defenses

To work towards wellness, you must leave control at the door and let go of your defenses.

Defenses are unconscious strategies that we all use to protect ourselves from painful, shameful, and fearful thoughts and feelings about ourselves. As protective structures, defenses provide a false sense of security. Allowing us to get through moments, our defenses and ego will make us believe that no more work is necessary. In a trauma, defense is the natural protective way for the body and mind to allow one to get through the trauma. It is a temporary fix, a survival skill. Unfortunately, the problem continues, because we often get stuck here. Then our defenses become embedded in our daily ways of being as if we are continually struggling. This becomes a familiar pattern and a standard way of being. For those with chronic and ongoing traumas, this may be the case. The problem is that once the traumas have left them, the body and mind continue to react as if the trauma is still occurring.

Here is an example: A child whose parents were not emotionally available may experience themselves as not loveable. "I was not good enough for my mom/dad to love me. Is that why they are gone all the time?" The child may socially isolate, keep to themselves, play alone, and put displaced feelings internally. Defensively, the child may regress by throwing a temper tantrum. The emotions and sensations of abandonment are associated with acting out, i.e., throwing a temper tantrum. The feelings and actions may translate into interpersonal relationships as they get older. When, as an adult, they experience a familiar experience of abandonment, they will resort to old defense patterns. The adult may throw an adult temper tantrum, i.e., grab the partner's keys so they can't leave the house, lock themselves in the bathroom, or even kick and scream. These patterns are continually repeating themselves over and over.

Negative self-talk

Another pattern that can repeat itself and cause damage is negative self-talk. If controlled, negative self-talk can be managed. Controlling negative self-talk means identifying statements or thoughts that bring you down, acknowledging them, and retraining for a positive mindset. For example, you can ask yourself, "If I am a compassionate person, how can I nourish that character?" or "How do I love and adore myself?" There are helpful techniques, and with practice, will move one from the emotions and sensations of

HEAL THY MIND

experiencing abandonment to understanding other ways to be rather than throwing a temper tantrum.

Forgiveness

Forgiveness List		
Mom	Dad	Children
Ex	Teacher	Friend
Enemy	Myself	Everyone

Establishing compassion is a process, and retraining your thoughts to a positive mindset is one path to a healthy lifestyle. You may also find healing through the process of forgiveness.

Some clinicians will disagree, saying that one does not need to forgive, especially in trauma cases. I think the ability or inability to forgive says more about you than your trauma—more about you than the person who hurt you. To me, forgiveness is a process of letting go. It is letting go of the negative self-talk, letting go of the grudges and bitterness that occupy space in your mind, blocking space for positive self-talk. Those negative aspects are like a bad relationship. You can't get rid of them. If you stay in the relationship, you may get sick and build up feelings of resentment, anger, and hatred. You are constantly activating your fight-flight-freeze response systems, which can increase your risk for heart disease, diabetes, depression, etc. Forgiveness is giving yourself a gift. After allowing conflicts and negative emotions and beliefs to leave you, you will release blockages, creating space for positive self-talk and healing.

Forgiveness is a conscious and deliberate decision to let go of resentments and control. Moving away from blaming and shaming, you move towards compassion and humility. Forgiveness is not about staying in an unhealthy relationship or trying to make a bad situation work; it is about setting limits and boundaries in a loving way. Releasing the old baggage, you are moving forward in your life without feeling defeated or ashamed and moving towards mental wellness.

Forgiveness is working towards controlling and destroying the ego, giving you opportunities for growth and self-care in a more profound way. Forgiveness is about you and not the other person. They did not win the fight. They did not get one over you. But you simply allow the anger and hatred to leave. In my life and in the stories that people have shared with me, I have found that forgiveness is complicated because of the belief we have that someone has done something wrong to us. I think Mother Theresa said it well: "It is not about the other. It is only about you and God."

When my dad dropped out of my life in sixth grade

and stopped adoring me as his little girl, I felt hurt and abandoned. I was angry. I struggled in high school and in life, trying to be accepted and loved. Finally, I reached out to him in college, trying to understand why he left me as a child. For me, the process of working through the hurt and beginning to release this pain took fifteen years. First, I had to be at a different point in my life to deal with all the abandonment issues. Then, when I was older, my father developed prostate cancer. I took care of him in his last months and days, which opened an opportunity for deep discussions. It was a humbling experience for both of us. Setting aside my issues, I needed to listen actively, hear him compassionately, and understand his perspective.

I began to understand that what he did in leaving me was out of fear. My father was raised in Louisiana; his family was a product of slavery. His great-great-grandfather was Caucasian and had procreated with the African slaves. In addition, women were sold if they were light-skinned. My father may have had some abandonment issues in his family history as well.

My dad was raised as a Jehovah's Witness since his birth. They don't celebrate holidays or birthdays. He'd get me an unwrapped gift, but it never said "Happy Birthday" on it. After listening to him, I saw that he was an excellent father who didn't know how to show it in the way I expected as a child. He needed to know he was forgiven. We gave him a clean bed and hired a caregiver to look after him. On the day he died, which was my birthday, we were gone for two to three hours while eating at a restaurant. He passed away while we were gone. That was his personality. He didn't want me to carry that burden on my birthday. As I was grieving, I went to a psychic who told me, "Your dad is telling me to tell you, 'Let me go.'" I also read a book co-authored by the Dalai Lama and the Archdiocese (see recommended resource section), which discussed grief and how forgiveness is about relationships. I could be that little girl my daddy adored. I lost that for a while, but I regained his love and trust at the end of his life. He gave me that gift. His voice is still embedded in me.

Kindness

I am a patient and loving mom.

Forgiveness and showing kindness go hand in hand, and, along with identifying triggers, they are helpful in developing mental wellness. Kindness allows you to focus on yourself and focus on others. Showing kindness boosts your mental state and your endorphins and brings calmness and encouragement. As you identify areas where you react, commonly known as triggers, you become more aware and can change how you react.

Try some of these practical methods of showing kindness:

1. Make flashcards of affirmations, create positive self-talk quotes, or use proverbs. Place them strategically in the house, for example, in the bathroom, on the refrigerator, or by the front door. Read them every time you pass them.
2. Make a screen saver of something you are working on that represents kindness for you. Example: "I want to work on being a better parent by being patient and listening more to my kids." The screen saver may have a specific picture of your kids with the caption "I am a patient mom/dad."
3. Write down a list of small things you can accomplish in a day. Put them on small pieces of paper in a jar. Each day, pick one up from the jar, such as "I will say three nice things to people at work," "I will call my

mom and let her vent about her day," or "I will be playful with my kids today."
4. Organize special holidays and celebrations (birthdays, anniversaries, significant events), and send people cards to let them know you were thinking about them.
5. Make gifts (and add special notes about the gifts) instead of buying items.
6. Have a conversation with someone different from you. Get to know someone. Challenge yourself and your beliefs.
7. Find time to volunteer in some meaningful way.
8. Smile and greet others as you walk by them.
9. Show up on time; be consistent and dependable; value your own time and other peoples'.
10. Buy a healthy meal or snack for someone and help and encourage someone to plant and grow their food.
11. Hug someone with permission. This releases oxytocin naturally. We all need a gentle touch.
12. Forgive the debt of someone who owes you money.
13. Pay for lunch for someone behind you in line or put coins in a meter that will expire.
14. Forgive someone else who may be driving in a rush as they cut you off.
15. Share your expertise with others free of charge. (4 & 5)

Takeaways

I forgive, accept, am kind and loving towards myself

Move towards a path of forgiveness, acceptance, kindness, and loving oneself. Your goal in life is to work on yourself, not to heal, cure, or treat others. You may guide them towards wellness, but they must do the work. The only true goal is for you to do your work. The ego is there to keep things in balance. Ultimately once in harmony, happiness can be achieved, then the ego is no longer needed. However, the ego desires to be needed to exist, so it will provide you with experiences in life so it can sustain itself. Learn to let things go. Remember, the work in life is your work. Taking care of the self is necessary. Learn to say "no" when things bring you out of balance and learn to say "yes" when things bring you into balance. You may experience both as unfamiliar and uncomfortable. To discover ways of creating balance, you could consider seeing a professional clinician, which brings us to Chapter 3: Therapy: Emotional and Mental Health.

Self-reflections

1. How can I take care of myself?
2. What is the inner, deeper work I need to do?
3. How can I forgive myself? Who did I need to forgive?
4. What are my struggles with being self-compassionate?
5. What are the healthy qualities of my ego, i.e., personality?
6. What is my daily self-care routine?
7. I will work on the following things this year to be loving and kind towards myself.

3

THERAPY: EMOTIONAL AND MENTAL HEALTH

P**roverb:** Where no counsel is, the people fall: but in the multitude of counsellors there is safety. (Christian Proverbs 11:14)

Affirmation: I am trusting; I am safe; I ask for help.

Let's work together

HEAL THY MIND

When I was a teenager, I struggled with depression. I was hurting after my daddy had suddenly left my life. I always tried to fit in; I longed to be accepted and wanted. Then, at age eighteen, when I was in college, I met a guy and fell head over heels in love with him—or what I thought was love. We ended up pregnant. In the first pregnancy, I had a miscarriage. The loss struck me hard. Becoming even more depressed, I thought about suicide and could barely function.

We became pregnant again, and I delivered a son. We were not getting along. But to provide a father figure and stability for my son, we stayed together. Both of us were inexperienced and young, each carrying our own anxiety and abandonment issues. Fearing he would leave me, I sometimes would hide his keys when he was trying to go out. We were fighting, throwing adult tantrums, and acting out our insecurities.

To help us resolve our conflict, we decided to see a therapist. She was an older woman, a "motherly type" who helped me sort out my feelings. It was my first encounter with counseling. Her teaching and method and the development of our relationship still impact me today. She gave me the freedom to make choices I didn't know I had. It was simple. She told me I could leave a "romantic" relationship because it was not healthy for me, and she also gave my partner the freedom to do the same. We separated, and I became a single parent, financially responsible for my son while studying in college. Quitting school was not an option. I persevered, graduating college with a 3.8 GPA and later pursuing my master's degree, all while raising my son and working to provide for him.

In my case, therapy gave me a range of tools to function and move towards wellness, happiness, and success. Therapy is helpful, especially when life is going well. We don't get distracted by daily struggles and can focus on a deeper understanding of thoughts, behaviors, feelings, reactions, and purpose. Therapy provides opportunities for growth and exploration. Therapy can help you dive deeper into your true authentic self. It can help you become aware of patterns and discover new ways of coping with life's struggles, stimulating wellness and hope.

I discovered that I enjoyed connecting with others when I was growing up. People were naturally attracted to me, often sharing their struggles and experiences with me in a natural, authentic way. Over the years as a clinician, I have developed an integrative approach to guiding people in their wellness journey. There are several treatment modalities to consider, including play therapy, cognitive behavior therapy, and psychodynamic and relational therapy. Trauma-sensitive yoga will also be discussed. These modalities are the ones I find most helpful in terms of trauma work.

Play therapy

Play therapy is helpful for both children (five years and older) and adults. For children, there is a limited ability to communicate through language in a meaningful way that expresses their thoughts, feelings, and experiences. Often things can be missed using language, because there are interruptions, misunderstandings, and struggles to find the words to articulate one's experience. Play is a concrete tool for children to express themselves in an emotionally safe way. The clinician must be trained with this modality to encourage, support, and understand the child's language. Play therapy can be used across genders and ethnic populations, because all children play.

Adults, especially those with trauma backgrounds, may not have had opportunities to play. If a parent does not know how to play with their children, those children also may be limited in their ability to play if no interventions are in place. Play mimics one's experiences in one's environment.

Why play therapy works

On the surface, it appears that play therapy is only about playing games, something like family game night. However, playing in treatment is different. The language and interventions are therapeutic. The goal in family game night may be to have fun, compete, and spend time together. The purpose of therapy is to facilitate healing, gain access to the child's inner world, and assist the child in feeling safe. Play therapy develops a sense of self-acceptance in the child, and this safe and trusting relationship helps access the child's inner world. (7)

Show me what your childhood was like

Reasons play therapy is effective

1. Play is the child's natural way of communicating. Children are not intellectual or verbal communicators. Therefore, play is in line with their development. Kids are not little adults with the total capacity to express and understand their feelings, thoughts, behaviors, and reactions. They are developing, and their brains are growing (only at age 25 is the brain fully developed). Play items such as toys, games, and activities are used as the child's words. Play is the child's natural way to engage with the world.

2. Children like to play, be active, and move around. Play activities relieve part of this discomfort when things are uncomfortable and challenging to talk about, process experiences in their body, and support the integration of these experiences. The whole child (mind-body-spirit) integration is activated. For example, a child working on anxiety will learn, practice, and eventually put language to their experiences through play. This supports and builds on the child's capacity to self-soothe (enhancing the mind-body-spirit integration that is formed in infancy), their capacity to self-regulate (which supports the practice of balancing mood experiences), and their self-initiative (which involves learning new material by freedom of choice in their play). Children can be curious about their world without the rules in place provided by parents, teachers, and other adults in their lives, engaging in relationships and activities in which they hold power. Play stimulates one's awareness of personality characteristics, skills, abilities, strengths, and challenges. While playing, children can explore cultural and ethnic differences, take pride in their work, and learn an appreciation for others. They can discover different situations and experiences and learn about their own family history and culture. While seeking and obtaining acceptance from peer groups, they can engage with and explore their

personal beliefs and experiment more with personal responsibility.
3. Children can be expressive and creative as symbolic scenarios/situations are created to resemble their emotional experiences. Play therapy provides opportunities for the clinician, sometimes in collaboration with the parents, to validate their children's experiences. In addition, they learn how to use language (verbal and nonverbal) to communicate their experiences to others. For example, language moves from anger to understanding how frustration, rage, and spite are on a spectrum of feelings.
4. The play space is adjustable. There are minimal rules, providing opportunities to be flexible, change, and adjust to what is going on in the moment. The clinician can start where the child/family is regarding treatment goals. Play changes depending on developmental needs and one's ability, accounting for religious, spiritual, cultural, and ethnic considerations. It supports everyone regardless of gender, economic status, etc.
5. Play supports physical development by engaging the body in sensory experiences, including experiences involving all five senses. For example, the child's movement brings awareness of changes in physical sensations within the body. In young children, specific movements can support and develop balance and

coordination. With teens, activities such as closing their eyes and standing on one foot can support different sensations that build on nerve connections in the body and brain. Implementing a play toolbox can help support their experiences in other environments—at home, school, and community.

6. Play stimulates cognitive development. Children learn to communicate with others, using language to understand and share their experiences. Expressive language, focusing on vocabulary and grammar, increases as they express their thoughts, feelings, and behaviors.

    Receptive language is enhanced in which children attend to, comprehend, and respond to others in complex ways. They learn the meaning of language. Speaking and listening, they discover their role as a participant in this exchange. They practice social and cultural rules of language.

7. Play supports spiritual development. Children explore their family, cultural, and community beliefs about the meaning of life. This includes broad categories of spirituality, faith, and religion. Children can understand their experiences, perceptions, and past opportunities through play depending on their developmental stage. When they are exposed to different play experiences, children are provided with opportunities to express and understand spiritual

parts of their development. Praying during a session, spiritual journaling, expressing forgiveness, and writing letters to God and sometimes other entities are examples of spiritual development connections. For young people, this process can produce intense emotions and result in finding ways to work through their conflictual experiences. (11)

Encouraging play

The child/teen is the leader in the session. There are no rules. I maintain the freedom to say things I don't like, because I am honest and authentic with a patient. However, I follow the child's lead once trust and safety are established. Yes, following their lead, and as the relationship develops, I find ways to integrate behavioral changes, saying, "I don't like to get hit in the face with Nerf bullets. I feel sad when you come to session high. I wonder what it would be like if you were to cry when you were sad instead of hit." I offer genuine praise and encouragement, different from a parent's role. I am honest about my experience with the child.

Compassionately, I provide choices and options. I encourage storytelling and am open to nontraditional forms of treatment if the child/teen wants to pursue these options, such as watching YouTube, learning music, or creating a skit. I support them, focusing on positive strengths by using language in the presence of the child's parent that demonstrates a different way to understand their behavior. I am silly; I laugh; I allow myself to be childlike. In my therapy office, I have a cooking area, arts and crafts, toy guns/weapons, books, a music area, dolls, a meditation/quiet area, and an area for yoga, exercise, or dance, all of which are available to stimulate play and work through trauma.

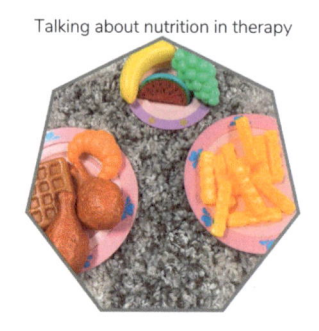

Talking about nutrition in therapy

Through play sessions, I am looking to understand the child/teen's experience in communicating and discovering their language. Asking reflective questions, I make interpretations based on what the child does or does not do during the session. For example, if a child chooses Legos in every session, this is a form of non-verbal communication. I assess the child's personality, demeanor, and interactions with peers/adults. I notice if they leave, go to the bathroom, or avoid eye contact, all of which suggest anxiety. I observe changes in physical posture that indicate confidence. I am also observing myself while in the child's presence, and I am thinking about the likeability of the child and how I enhance the child's strengths and explain them to others.

An example is a boy who only wanted to play with Legos when he came into the office. At first, he sat rigidly, stacking and ordering the Legos. He rarely spoke; he just played with the Legos. He needed to have complete control over every action. Then, over several months, he began to feel safe. He relaxed and shared more about his home environment, which he felt was chaotic and unconnected. Through playing with Legos, he was able, with my help, to process what he was feeling and experiencing, and I guided him to make choices about better ways of coping.

Cognitive-Behavioral Therapy

What Thought, Feeling, Emotion is expressed

Besides implementing play therapy to help patients, I use cognitive-behavioral therapy or CBT. CBT helps a person to understand their thoughts, feelings, and behaviors. This modality is based on discovering faulty and negative thinking patterns. Some of these thinking and behavioral patterns are learned from parents, and others are learned in the child's environment. The idea is to identify the thinking and behavioral errors and then learn techniques to unlearn these patterns and replace them with helpful and positive thinking patterns. By learning to control thoughts, individuals can gain the ability to direct their thoughts in a particular way. If the thought is "I am stupid and will never complete this book," then I will feel discouraged, and I may sleep more or distract myself from my book writing days. I can change this thought to "Although it may be difficult, I can work on and finish this book. I am a good writer with helpful information to share." If I think this way, then I will feel inspired, and, in turn, complete the book.

Cognitive-behavioral therapy helps patients in the following ways. First, it allows patients to understand their own thought process better. Second, it helps them to understand the thinking errors. Third, it helps them to make choices about change. For example, if a teen says, "My parents hate me because I get in trouble a lot," then I offer other perspectives. Their thoughts come from a place of abandonment, shame, and low self-esteem. Reframing their perspective, I try to challenge the patterns. (10). I have worksheets and flashcards that look at broad thinking patterns, highlighting specific and individual thinking errors. If the person wants to change, then I can bring awareness and help them to practice new habits. In future sessions, I reinforce the idea that their parents love them. "Your mom texted me yesterday and told me you passed your math class. She must be proud of you."

Psychodynamic theory

Helping clients understand new perspectives is also the goal of psychodynamic theory, the broader category of relational therapy. We all struggle with feeling that we are disconnected from others in life. Psychological challenges occur when disconnections arise in our relationships. Our earliest relationships in life are with parents/caregivers; these relationships are the foundation for all our future relationships. When a child is born, attachments are formed to people and objects. Attachment is a reciprocal relationship between adult and child. If we were secure in our relationship with our primary caregiver—i.e., if they were attentive to our needs, understood us when we cried, welcomed us, and celebrated as we came into the world—then we will be similarly secure in our future relationships. Those who are secure are close with their parents and have no separation anxiety, but they are also confident and can regulate boundaries. As an adult, one is comfortable around other people and alone and behaves in a loving and supportive way.

The same principle applies if we were unwanted or felt unloved. Our relationships in the future will be a series of reactions and triggers that arise in us. If a child has a parent who is depressed or a workaholic, then the child will not seek closeness in relationships and may withdraw.

Hard to console, the child may throw temper tantrums

and experience separation anxiety. As they grow into adults, they may be emotionally unavailable, i.e., unable to express emotions and repeating patterns passed on by their parents. An adult who experienced a lack of love in childhood may fear abandonment and suffer intense anxiety, exhibiting clingy behavior and mood swings.

Working through these issues and helping patients to find secure attachment is the goal of therapy. There is a parallel process with treatment. The infant-parent relationship mimics the patient-clinician relationship. In the latter case, the clinician is the trained expert and can support the patient to work through unresolved unconscious material from infancy. Helping the patient develop a balanced ego, the clinician should provide safety, trust, and consistency and should have a balanced ego to support the patient. There are usually three entities in the clinical room: me with all the stuff I bring, my patient with all the stuff they bring, and the interaction between us. This is the therapeutic relational relationship.

During these series of interactions, many things are being repeated, and these patterns are observed and explored. I often refer to this process as enactments fueled by unconscious psychic forces within the patient and the clinician. The clinician, at specific points, may take on the reminders of the abuse/trauma, providing space for the patient to work through this unconscious and conscious material. It is a dramatic scene in the treatment office where certain parts of the patient's story will be acted out.

HEAL THY MIND

Early relationships shape a person's experiences and understanding of themselves in relation to others and the world. People create and engage in patterns in terms of beliefs, behaviors, feelings, and reactions to situations. These patterns are both unconscious and conscious and are repeated over and over. In therapy sessions, the clinician and the patient will explore these patterns, which will be recreated, noticed, discussed, and understood. Therapy brings what is hidden from the individual into conscious awareness, giving opportunities for the patient to reflect on what they feel, think, and want to do about the pattern. Awareness can bring about change, moving subconscious material into conscious awareness. (9)

Adjunctive practice to the treatment

I also use trauma-sensitive yoga to support my patients in conjunction with psychodynamic theory, cognitive behavior therapy, and play therapy. Trauma-sensitive yoga uses focused breathing to connect the conscious and the subconscious minds. It is a mind-body-spirit connection. I will invite you to notice sensations, experiment with different breathing techniques, and make choices that feel useful and help you to stay present, allowing your body to inform your decisions. Curiosity helps create emotional distance in which people can "just notice" their internal states without taking immediate action to shift these states. David Emerson said, "My body holds the trauma stories of others" (8). That is why I practice trauma-sensitive yoga consistently. Yoga consists of breathwork, physical movement, and a meditative state of being. The trauma part is understanding trauma theory and its implications on the mind-body-spirit interconnection.

Using a bottom-up approach to work on the body, trauma-sensitive yoga understands that consistency and reliability are essential and focuses on the needs of the individual. The practice is adaptable, not prescribing a set of rules and regulations. The process involves grounding, self- regulating, accepting, and reconnecting. Simply, trauma- sensitive yoga allows the patient to explore, having an experience with no expectation or judgment.

As a relational integrative therapist, I am highly skilled in various treatment modalities that I use in the treatment room. My patients don't fit into a box, and neither do I. As a child, I was never one to color within the lines. I didn't follow all the rules, and I questioned my teachers all the time. People have various needs, underlying issues, and complexities. Always reaching into my clinical toolbox, I collaborate with my patient to find the way towards wellness, happiness, and success. I try to provide alternatives to addressing one's mental wellness, because suffering is unnecessary. I don't believe that people are sick or ill; I believe people are hurting and reacting to traumas. They are trying to figure out life with limited tools, which is why I created the OCTAVES method.

Your life is like a puzzle. There are thousands of pieces. You have tried to put the puzzle together. You may start by matching pieces based on color or shape. I am also working with you on your puzzle. I may start with the frame on the outside. As we work together, we are putting the puzzle together. Sometimes you will get triggered, because I put a puzzle piece in the wrong space. Sometimes I will observe how you understand the puzzle process and bring things to your attention. I will say, "I noticed some irritation. What do you think that may be about?"

As we continue, we work together to assemble the puzzle. In addition to this co-creation, I will bring things into the treatment. I will explore stuff that doesn't appear related to our work on the puzzle. This helps to rule out other possibilities. For example, functional medicine tells us to look at mold, pesticides, environmental toxins, nutritional deficiencies, and other issues that can be underlying causes of depression, anxiety, schizophrenia, ADHD, autism, etc. I also use bioenergetic healing as an alternative to traditional psychiatric medications.

I am an innovator in the practice of this form of integration. Instead of treating illness or disease, I help those who want to move towards wellness, happiness, and success and know more about their options, challenge their deep-rooted beliefs about themselves and others, and question their behaviors and reactions to situations. I discuss the importance of nutrition. I encourage them to move their bodies. I explore concepts relating to spirituality, religion, faith, and nonfaith. I would say that the person can heal themselves and that we work together on finding ways that are meaningful to them in this journey.

Qualifications of a clinician

As a clinician, I work on myself to be the healthiest version of myself that I can. I cannot bring my baggage into the therapy room. I am grounded and do lots of self-care, practicing what I write about in this book. I am at a good place, allowing me to hear my clients' deep-rooted underlying experiences and reflections. This helps patients in several ways.

1. Patients can work on their stuff without my stuff coming out. Patients can care for themselves and not feel the need to care for me.
2. The focus is on them. I encourage moments of self-disclosure. This is purposeful and intentional; it supports the patient in moving forward with treatment and feeling connected but not meeting my needs.
3. I offer a nonjudgmental space and reassurance that there is no shaming or blaming. I encourage their discussions of the most intimate, private parts of their life.

4. I work to reframe their experiences and find ways to push them to reflect deeply about their internal affairs.
5. I thank them for their courage and appreciate their time in the session.

Breakthroughs

My patients commonly experience progress, but it is never the same. When a hard decision is made to start this progress, growth happens, and it is challenging. I am not talking about mandated or forced clients, but those who want real deep life change for themselves. Therapy is one part of the process, encouraging patients to learn more about what is going on and make the unknown known. This is an amazing process that I have experienced both as a clinician and as a patient. As a clinician, I am glad to have been a small part of a person's growth. As a patient, it has been eye-opening for me. Therapy is beneficial in helping people to find healing, hope, and a sense of wellbeing.

HEAL THY MIND

Takeaways

Meet Piggy, She keeps your worries away

There was likely a period in life when you were happy. Some people must go far back into their childhood, and others may not recall these times of happiness. To understand yourself as you move towards wellness, it is crucial to understand your childhood, relationships, and these early experiences in life. They helped to shape your personality. Look for patterns that you are recreating in life, in your relationships, and with your emotions. This most complicated work done in therapy is often the least discussed and most avoided. Find a trained professional you can connect with, even if it costs money. Your mental awareness and mental success needs a professional perspective. Know that the process takes time to unravel

HEAL THY MIND

all the stuff that moved one towards being sick, ill, or diseased. It also takes time to rediscover, repair, replenish, and succeed in healing thy mind. Besides implementing connections and healing through therapy, well-being can also be achieved through play and childlike activity, which will be discussed in the next chapter of Animal: Playful Inner Health.

Self-reflections

1. What do I want to gain from therapy?
2. What are the therapeutic goals I set for myself?
3. What does my commitment look like for my healing?
4. Am I ready to start this journey, considering that it is a major commitment in terms of both time and money?
5. How do I prepare my friends, family, and loved ones for my change?
6. What has prompted me to want to start this process now?
7. What am I willing and unwilling to do to be an active participant in my healing?

4

ANIMAL: PLAYFUL INNER HEALTH

Proverb: To cry and not be carried away by tears, to laugh and not be carried away by laughter, is the way. (Taoism)

Affirmation: There are goofy and fun parts of myself that I share with others.

I start many of my sessions with my younger patients playing and behaving in a childlike way. If a patient likes basketball, we may shoot hoops in the exercise room. If a patient is into crafting, we may paint or color or create. If building is important, we may stack Legos for hours, as the child shares their stories about his/her life. My therapy dogs also offer support in sessions as people process their experiences and move towards wellness, happiness, and success.

In my sessions with adults, I am childlike in another way. I listen to the language of the patient. I encourage emotional expression as a sign of strength. This includes laughing, doing weekly check-ins, crying, and showing irritation and even anger and frustration. These expressions of emotions are superficial and provide space for the patient to begin doing the work needed to move them towards mental wellness.

In this chapter, we will explore why play boosts our mental health, the stages of childhood play, the benefits of play, how play has changed, the importance of setting limits on tech time, the importance of playing outside, how adults can rediscover their inner child, and how therapy animals support the healing process.

HEAL THY MIND

Playful inner health

Playfulness is at the core of who we are. It means letting go of that voice that judges you, shames you, and tells you, "You can't." It is sometimes our parents' voice, sometimes our bosses, and sometimes a friend's voice. Many times it is our own voice. We were born into a world at some point, and we were happy. For some, being in our mother's belly is when the trauma started; for others, it was during childhood or adolescence. However, there was a point for most of us, if we go far back, when we were happy. When you ask children what they want to be when they grow up, you don't usually hear "a drug addict," "a child abuser," "a pedophile," or "a terrorist." Instead, something happens along the path. This was when the imbalances began—maybe the abuses, the struggles with personality dysfunction, or negative cognitive distortions. We get lost. Without supportive, nurturing, and dependable adults to support us, we continue the pattern of being lost. We lose the playful part of ourselves. Sometimes these disruptions began so early in our lives that play stops because of other family obligations. Sometimes play stops because of trauma. Sometimes play stops because of a parent's limitations. Sometimes play stops because of a loss of resources, environmental concerns, etc.

We know that children are playing less, and that the rates of anxiety and depression are increasing. Playing is vitally

HEAL THY MIND

essential to health. The focus is on being "childlike," not "childish."

There's a difference. "Childlike" promotes positive and complementary qualities such as honesty, purity, and innocence. The ability to trust others, someone who is childlike, is full of energy, excitement, and enthusiasm. They are curious to discover new interests and sources of enjoyment.

"Childish" has a negative sense or association and includes foolish, annoying, and immature forms of behavior. Your emotions can escalate; the focus is on someone else. Someone who is childish exhibits attention-seeking behavior, lies, covers up behaviors and avoids punishment.

BE CHILDLIKE: NOT CHILDISH

Stages of play

To understand the importance of childlike play, one must grasp the stages of play in children. Around 0–3 months, an infant will make movements with arms, legs, hands, and feet. In addition, they are learning about their bodies with certain movements. A toddler from birth to two years will play alone, trying to figure out how things work and observing reactions and responses from others. By two years of age, the child will watch others play and observe how they play. Next, the child will start to play with others near them. The child around three and four years old will demonstrate some interaction during their play. They may not engage in the same activity as other children but will engage in an activity near other children's play. By four, the child mimics and engages in play with other children. There is interest in one activity and playing in a cooperative sequential fashion.

Play is crucial to a child's development. It supports the natural stages of development essential for life and allows the child to practice behaviors by imitating adults. In addition, it supports their understanding and adjustment to their environment—socially, emotionally, physically, and spiritually. (12)

HEAL THY MIND

Benefits of play

1. Relieves stress. It releases endorphins (feel-good chemicals in the body), promotes an overall sense of well-being, and provides temporary relief from some pains.
2. Keeps the brain active. Engaging in activities like chess, puzzles, and task- and memory-related games help to exercise the brain and muscles and defend against depression.
3. Encourages creative expression. This is not restricted to the right side of the brain but includes three distinct brain networks: (1) the default network, which is related to brainstorming and daydreaming; (2) the executive control network, which is stimulated when focus is required; (3) the salience network, which can detect environmental stimuli and movement across executive and default networks.
4. Supports a secure attachment both in children and adults. Interpersonal relationships are encouraged. Spending playful time with someone brings on an overall sense of joy and satisfaction in relationships with others. This is the reason why some children and teens appreciate and welcome relationships with peers, as they get to play together.
5. Keeps your body in movement, giving you more energy and improving overall health.

HEAL THY MIND

6. Helps to bring the mind-body-spirit into balance.
7. Releases emotional traumas from the past. It gives you space to work through your trauma in a nonverbal way. (15 & 16)

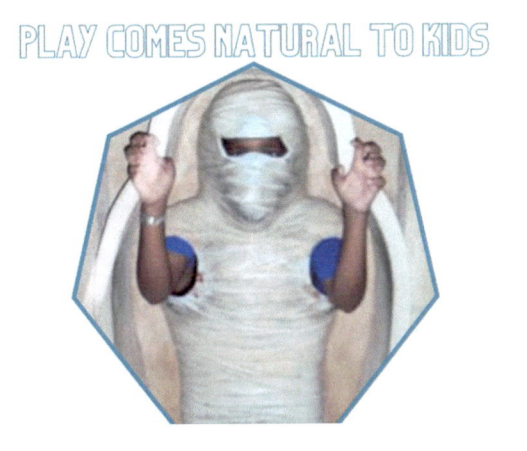

PLAY COMES NATURAL TO KIDS

How play has changed

Over the years, the way children play has changed.

- There is less in-person, face-to-face contact.
- We have access to more information.
- More families have Internet access and cell phones.
- Kids have transitioned from outdoors to indoors, and the use of screen time has increased with the rise of social media and other electronic media.
- Kids have more access to other adults (e.g., drivers and food delivery people).

- Books can be in the form of verbal and written expression.
- There is greater pressure at schools, which have become more competitive.
- People play fewer board games and more electronic games.
- Friendships are developed online.
- Fathers are more actively involved in parenting and disciplining.
- Children are living in more than one home-like environment.
- Kids can create things faster and with less material.
- Kids are exposed to various home-like environments with peers across the world.
- Kids may play with Barbies both in their playhouse and online.
- Boys may learn to skate with a skateboard in the front yard and through YouTube videos.

Just because things are changing, it does not mean that they are changing for the better or the worse. They are just changing, and adapting to changing play can be a helpful and a positive experience. As we continue to change as a society, our expectations should change.

HEAL THY MIND

Screen time benefits and setting limits

With the increase in screen time, it is important to examine the benefits. We can use technology to support adaptation to the real world. Some digital tools and apps can connect families. There is real-time access to resources and support. Parents can learn to use tools that encourage their child's cognitive, emotional, social, and linguistic development even at a young age. This can increase the child's readiness for school, promote the teen's adaptability, support family bonding, and provide the means to stay connected in other meaningful ways in a child's life. Now children can sustain connections from early childhood into adulthood.

While recognizing the benefits of screen use, parents should balance technology time.

1. Have specific times and time limits for screen time. For example, avoid meaningful conversations with children when distracted by screens.
2. Have intentional screen-free moments (e.g., meals, driving in the car, family night).
3. Avoid blue light, which is emitted on screens, in nighttime routines. Engage your child's interest with screen time activities instead of allowing them to do this alone. Be curious about what they are doing and encourage them to play outside.

Playing outside

Playing outside is vital for healthy living. Vitamin D is essential for many body processes, including the immune system, brain development, mood regulation, and bone development.

Exercise gives opportunities for the child to be active and to move during the day. Being outside supports these activities. They learn to negotiate with others, solve problems, and plan, organize, and participate in play, a form of multitasking. Besides managing anxieties, they can learn to separate themselves from their parents/caregivers. They learn about safety and trust in others. They take risks, and as they become teenagers, their risks can be more intense (at least for adults). Playing is another way of building social relationships. Through play, young people learn to make, sustain, and separate from peer relationships. They learn to cooperate, share, argue, and disengage from others and situations. There is an appreciation for outdoor activities, nature, changes in day to night, and earth.

HEAL THY MIND

Adults discover their inner child

WHAT STAGE OF PLAY ARE YOU

Playing triggers parts of the creative aspects of the brain. It releases hormones to relieve stress. It improves memory and brain function, which is why patients play (color, arts & crafts, and sing) at nursing homes. It teaches you a new skill and encourages you to stay engaged with yourself and others. Playing prevents boredom, providing other opportunities for growth outside of mindless activities, such as watching TV. For example, I taught myself to knit. To learn this new skill, I went to events and watched videos. I had to read about, think about, and engage in knitting, all of which involved mind-body-spirit. My cognition was activated because I learned and created new patterns. I was physically engaged, moving my hands in unfamiliar ways. I explored my purpose and the usefulness of knitting, connecting with the spiritual aspects of my being.

Here are some ideas to become childlike:

- Engage in an activity in which you can fully play.
- Be playful in relationships with coworkers, with pets, and with children. Use your imagination, be creative, increase your problem-solving abilities, and allow yourself to express your emotions. Kids do it. Adults can, too.
- Dress up for a holiday, such as Halloween, or host a superhero party.
- Have a tea party with some friends.
- Play in the snow. Have a snowball fight and attempt to make a snowman/woman.
- Teach your pet a trick.
- Have an online or in-person charade party.
- Go skating, cycling, or swimming.
- Read or listen to a silly kids' story.
- Have a sleepover, share stories, and tell scary stories.
- Engage in a hobby with other adults, laugh, and have fun.

In addition to play therapy, emotional support, pets, and therapy animals can also support mental health.

Emotional support animals

In most states, a mental health professional can write letters for emotional support animals (ESA). A pet can be an emotional support to a human. ESAs are pets that often live with individuals, providing emotional support to humans. I look for certain demeanors when selecting an animal, and I observe the relationship between the owner and the animal, but specialized training is not required. The animal is simply there to help the person cope. Emotional support animals cannot travel without other approvals and do not get third-party accommodations or other things covered under the American Disabilities Act. ESAs are domesticated animals, such as dogs, cats, pigs, rabbits, guinea pigs, snakes, horses, and birds. The pets must be manageable outdoors and in public areas, and they must have a controllable demeanor. (13)

Benefits of ESAs

Emotional support animals provide many benefits for their owners.

1. Pets increase communication between the brain and body. Dopamine and neurochemicals can increase when pets are around. This raises one's capacity to love and show affection. In addition, pets increase

the production of antibodies in the body, helping to improve immune function.
2. Pets bring calmness and reduce anxiety, especially when a person is in a distressing situation, such as getting blood drawn or traveling on an airplane.
3. Pets bring a sense of companionship, especially when lonely. This is because they provide physical contact, a form of cuddling.
4. Most of the time, pets provide unconditional love and affection to their owner(s). They may be protective of their owner, responding when their owner is sad or angry. At times, the pets' reaction is authentic, and their owners can change their behavior to avoid distressing their pets. The pet helps the owner to notice emotional dysregulations and triggers.
5. Pets can be used as a therapeutic tool to improve self-esteem, set boundaries, and follow the rules, encouraging their owners to demonstrate patience, engage in healthy eating, and participate in outdoor activities and exercise.
6. Pets can support someone struggling with outdoor activities, socializing, engaging with others (by giving adults and kids something to talk about), and nervousness.
7. Pets can keep one emotionally grounded. For example, the ESA can remain calm and focused when the owner is agitated, encouraging the owner to do the same.

Therapy animals

Like ESA animals, therapy dogs can help people move towards wellness, happiness, and success. A therapy dog is a certified trained animal that works with its owner to address specific target areas. These pets have a certain demeanor and usually include dogs, cats, and horses. Therapy animals complete training programs, including basic and advanced classes. Therapy dogs must tolerate being around other pets, people of all ages, and individuals who use supports, such as wheelchairs, crutches, and walking sticks. They should remain relatively calm when asked to do so, especially during therapy moments, and become active when requested to do so on command. A therapy dog can be an emotional support animal to the owner, but an emotional support animal is not necessarily a therapy animal. With some training, the dog's demeanor should be friendly, obedient, calm, unaggressive (even if its tail is pulled), gentle, relaxed (unless given a command to respond differently), and not easily startled. A therapy dog is assessed based on its temperament, how much it sheds (my Husky needed weekly combs), its sociality, and its adaptability to different environments. (14)

I have worked with two therapy dogs. The first one, Summer, is a medium-sized Chihuahua mix and a beagle. She worked with patients to calm them during anxious moments and supported emotional expressions of sadness and depression. She helped them through the therapy process, which often indicated to me what type of work was needed in the session.

I have a lovely story about a patient's recovery from depression. Summer started off close to the patient, and then after a year, as the patient's symptoms decreased, Summer provided distance by moving in the other room. Like many therapy dogs, when Summer was not needed, she left. This back and forth happened a few times, and eventually, the patient's depressive symptoms were minimal.

My current therapy dog is a large, furry, blue-eyed Husky named Mona. She works primarily with children struggling with rules, hyperactivity, focus, low confidence, poor eating habits, grief, loss, anxiety, and trauma. Here is a funny story about shedding. Mona did not have a lot of combing during COVID. After months, when she did get brushed, it was in the office. The entire front office was filled with her hair. It took weeks to get the hair off the floor and furniture. It was a husky blizzard in my office for a few months.

These dogs are my pets, and although they are trained, they are still animals. Mona may jump and get excited around kids and adults. Summer barks a lot when children run and get active. Dogs are valuable tools in the therapy environment. You will hear about past experiences of animals—pets who died, pets who were given away, pets who were hated, pets who attacked others, and animal abuse—from children, teens, and sometimes adults. Most patients are happy for Mona to be present during our sessions. Keep in mind a clinician should consistently assess for any allergies and inquire about comfort or discomfort around animals.

Patients always have the option to ask for Mona to go into another room, and Mona also has an opportunity to go into another room. I often call this a time-out. Sometimes Mona goes to group homes to spend time with other children and teens. She loves the attention and affection, and they do too.

I use a parallel process in therapy sessions. Mona goes to school and has homework; so do the children. Mona eats carrots, other veggies and fruits, and drinks lots of water like humans are encouraged to do. Mona sometimes gets frustrated and tired and needs to self-regulate and put herself on a time-out. Mona enjoys being with others and enjoys alone time. Mona gets sick and needs love and affection.

As her trainer and dog mom, I spend quality time together with Mona engaged in activities, training, and reinforcement (homework). We attend parties and events together. We are affectionate with each other. I am mimicking an authentic experience for parents and showing how they can work on the quality of their parenting.

THERAPY DOGS

Benefits of a therapy dog

Implementing a therapy dog can have many benefits.

1. The dog is specifically trained to work on targeted treatment goals.
2. Can relieve immediate anxiety, decrease blood pressure, and encourage a relaxed state for some patients.
3. Useful to those who don't have pets. It is like having a pet without responsibilities all the time.
4. Uses nonverbal ways to communicate with a patient, teaching calmness, gentleness, and patience. Encourages communication, developing and empowering the patient's voice.
5. Encourages self-regulation, emotional expression, and unconditional love. Provides a non-judgmental relationship for the individual.

6. Supports communication about trauma, providing opportunities to talk about abuse, neglect, trauma, depression, anxiety, family challenges, and behavioral problems.
7. Encourages exercise and movement of one's body. The patient is more likely to engage with a therapy dog than alone.

There are many examples of how therapy dogs help patients.

- An elderly patient had severe trauma due to being shot. At the beginning of a session, Summer would sit next to her closely. As the client rubbed Summer, she would cry. Summer was helping the woman work through her emotions. Over time, Summer would move away and then come close again if the client began to cry again. The woman started regulating her mood and improving her mental state, working towards wellness. There was a beautiful transition over many sessions.
- Another story is of a young girl who experienced trauma and was quite shy, with low self-confidence. She kept to herself. Mona helped to build her confidence. If Mona came too close, the girl had to learn to say, "Move!" in her big girl voice. Then, finding her voice and confidence, she learned to be stern, take control, and give orders.

- A teen girl experienced trauma when his mother and father died. In the session, she would lay with Mona and cry. At times, I laid on the floor with both of them. Then Mona and her would get up and run around the office. It gave her space to talk about her experiences. It flowed naturally as she interacted with Mona. She would place Mona's paw on her neck in the form of a hug. Mona would let her cry. The girl eventually shared memories of her parents and her dogs, who also died as part of her tragic experience.
- Elderly parents were concerned about their 45-year-old homeless son's suffering from symptoms associated with schizophrenia. He was disheveled, had poor hygiene, and was often unmotivated. His parents forced him into therapy. In the session, he received healthy snacks and water. However, Mona did not come to him initially; she was standoffish and avoided him. I had to learn her language, like a parent needs to know a child's language. While observing sessions and exploring why Mona was acting this way, I realized it was because of his poor hygiene. Once this was discussed in treatment, things slowly changed. He slowly came into the session with a different presentation. He showered and dressed in clean clothes. He improved his hygiene and sometimes even used too much cologne. Mona started to get physically closer to him. Then they

HEAL THY MIND

shared healthy snacks in sessions. Impressed with his progress and changes, his parents decided to get him an emotional support animal. The animal gave him a sense of purpose and accomplishment, keeping him motivated to be hygienic and to get outside for walks. He took the dog to puppy class, which provided social engagement.

All these stories illustrate how play, combined with the other methods, encourages wellness, happiness, and success. It is also essential to eat a nutritious diet, which we will explore in the next chapter, Victuals: Nutritional Health.

HEAL THY MIND

Takeaways

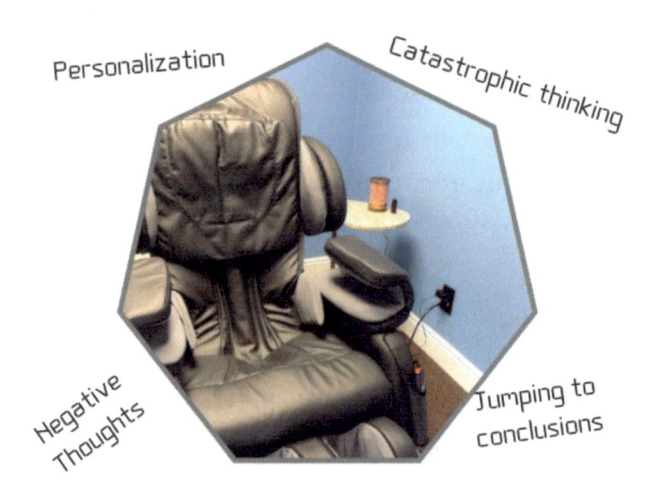

Personalization

Catastrophic thinking

Negative Thoughts

Jumping to conclusions

Learn the difference, and practice being childlike and not childish. I challenge you to find the deep part of you that laughs, spreads joy, and brushes things off. Heal and forgive the inner child within. Play is not only crucial for children, but also for adults. Be flexible and open to new experiences, and you may surprise yourself and build confidence. Rediscovering nature and connecting with animals can benefit your emotional wellness. Animals provide this nonverbal means of supporting emotional attachments, especially if one struggles with early childhood traumas and attachment challenges.

Self-reflections

1. What type of play did you enjoy as a child?
2. How can you adapt the play you did as a child to play as an adult?
3. What can you do to encourage more fun and laughter in your life?

4. What animal do you think closely relates to your personality?
5. How can having pets/animals around you help improve your health?
6. If you have a pet, what are some activities you can do with your pet that improve your mental health and your pet's health?
7. What are you willing to do outside your everyday activities? Go to a bird show or learn to bird-watch. Go to the zoo and watch the behavior of the animals. Learn to skate, cycle, or run with your pet. Spend time at a cat café. Learn to draw and imitate a dolphin. Volunteer at an equestrian center.

5
VICTUALS: NUTRITION HEALTH

Proverb: The body becomes what the foods are, as the spirit becomes what the thoughts are. (Ancient Egyptian proverb)

Affirmation: I make healthy choices. I love veggies and herbs. I eat to detoxify and nourish my mind, body, and spirit.

HEAL THY MIND

Making healthy choices in eating can boost your immune system and stimulate healing in your body and mind. This chapter will explore the benefits of a vegan lifestyle, discuss nutrient-filled vegetables, proteins, herbs, fruits, and nuts, suggest foods to avoid, and recommend supplements.

After my son's father and I separated, I began juggling the responsibilities of college, raising my son as a single parent and working. I graduated from college and worked different jobs—one was at a forensic facility, servicing people with mental illnesses, addiction issues, and pedophiles. With those interactions, I became protective of my son, who was a little boy at the time. These jobs also pushed me to pursue my master's degree, in which I graduated at the top of my class. With all the stress, I began veering towards a path of unhealthy choices, eating junk food (a lot of starches) and drinking up to a gallon of milk a day. Depressed and struggling, I sometimes could not get out of bed. My diet fluctuated, and I didn't sleep well. Adding to all the anxiety, my son's father became increasingly violent towards me. He threatened me and exhibited angry behaviors, such as scratching my car. Once, he hit me after I made a sarcastic comment at a family gathering in his father's home. I had to request a restraining order against him. The stress was beginning to take its toll and affect my health. I gained more weight. At one point in my mid-thirties, I weighed 240 pounds. I had gut issues and was hypoglycemic and obese. Sometimes I would faint and get lightheaded. I hated going to doctors because of their emphasis on treating disease with drugs instead of addressing the underlying issues. I wanted to find more natural ways of healing.

As my symptoms got worse, I decided to see a naturopathic doctor. That doctor recommended that I stop eating gluten. No more pasta, which I enjoyed. It was suggested to give up meats and dairy too. Test results showed nodules on my throat. That doctor referred me to an endocrinologist, who said the nodules looked precancerous. He also diagnosed me with Hashimoto's Disease and recommended I start taking thyroid medicine. He said that if I were placed on thyroid medicine, I would have to take it for the rest of my life. The diagnosis was life changing. I knew if I did not make changes in my health, I would be heading down a destructive path. So, refusing the doctor's advice to take thyroid medication, I changed my eating habits, first moving towards vegetarianism and then veganism.

Nutrition is so vital to addressing underlying issues. I went back to the doctor two years later, and tests indicated that the nodules had disappeared. Knowing I was not on medication, the doctor dismissed me and my results after discovering that I was vegan. Setting his opinion aside, I focused on improving my mental and physical health. I went from being suicidal and depressed to wondering why my life was so great. I am a better caregiver to myself. If I am the healthiest version of myself; it flows out to everyone else. I feel great. I am not stressed.

Working with trauma patients, I give small suggestions to help them move towards mental and physical wellness, happiness, and eventually their success. One of these suggestions is moving to a vegetarian/vegan lifestyle, which focuses on a plant-based diet and minimizes and/or avoids animal products, including meat, dairy, and eggs.

I have been vegetarian off and on for most of my adult life, transitioning to being vegan in 2016. I started transitioning to a raw vegan diet in 2019. The transition to a raw diet, like all transitions, is a challenge for most. You need to retrain the body, brain, and spirit. My suggestion is to start off slow, with no drastic changes. I gave myself a year to get dairy out of my system, and cheese was the last thing to go. I made sure I was prepared by pre-packing food: I had food in my purse, car, and work. It was accessible. I limited myself from going out to eat. Preparing my food choices, I switched my diet based on the seasons (fall, winter, spring, and summer) for various nutrients.

To keep my diet balanced, I made sure I got all six tastes in my meals daily—sweet, sour, salty, pungent (spicy), bitter, and astringent. I worked to limit my consumption of sweet and salty and move towards more pungent and bitter to help with the detoxifying process.

Additionally, I prepared meals that were more consistent with a high alkaline diet. Taking cooking classes, learning new recipes, and joining other raw vegan communities were ways to educate myself. I read various books to help support the transition, talked more with farmers, and took a few tours. I have co-created meals so tasty that I have been amazed, and I have created meals that I would not eat again. I limited my time watching TV, especially commercials, to help me stay focused. Now, keep in mind that I am still in transition. I work on my thoughts and food preparation. For me, this is not only a behavioral change but a spiritual transformation. I believe I am "God-like," and I want to consume physical-mental-spiritual foods that honor God.

Benefits of Vegan Lifestyle

There are many benefits of being vegan/vegetarian and eating healthily. A vegan lifestyle has the following benefits:

1. Regulates and increases energy.
2. Relieves stress on your immune system.
3. Improves or eliminates chronic illness.
4. Weight loss/weight maintenance.
5. Regulates and eases menstrual cycle (hormones from dairy are known to increase fibroids, cysts, and endometriosis in women).
6. Increases longevity and improves the quality of life (the oldest people globally have a whole food, organic lifestyle, with about 97% vegan).
7. A vegan lifestyle is more cost-effective on a long-term basis.

As you transition to a healthier lifestyle, I recommend a diet enriched with fruit and vegetables. Again, it can be helpful to see a professional as you transition. In addition, you can work towards having more of your diet come from natural organic sources. I work towards a 70/30 rule, which means eating 70% raw and 30% cooked, but the overall goal is to move towards simple whole organic fruits and vegetables. Here are the foods to consider, with information about how they can assist body functioning. We will discuss vegetables, proteins, herbs, fruits, and nuts. We will also explore foods to avoid, including processed sugar, sodium, fat, dairy, and meat.

Vegetables

A vegetable is a plant or part of a plant used for food consumption. (34) Vegetables should be rich in sulfur, chlorophyll, fiber, vitamins A, B, and C, and antioxidants to support detoxification. (30) Examples are onion, garlic, beets, dandelion root, ginger, carrot, wheatgrass, broccoli, cayenne pepper, artichoke, kale, romaine lettuce, seaweed, watercress, cabbage, celery, collard greens, parsley, and cucumber.

To support the digestive system, nutrient-dense vegetables are essential. This list includes kale, broccoli, cauliflower, spinach, Brussels sprouts, onions, carrots, sweet potatoes, bell peppers, asparagus, microgreens, collard greens, turnip and mustard greens, sea vegetables, bell peppers, and green peas.

Alkaline vegetables help to balance internal functioning. This list includes spinach, kale, collard greens, Swiss chard, broccoli, arugula, Brussel sprouts, Bok Choy, sweet potato, beets, cauliflower, carrots, celery, asparagus (24).

Proteins

Spirulina and alfalfa are good sources of protein as well. Proteins include lentils, chickpeas, beans, nutritional yeast, hempseed, green peas, quinoa, chia seeds, and nuts. A complete source of protein encompasses approximately 20 different amino acids. The body can produce nine on its own. The protein must contain all nine of the essential amino acids in equal amounts to be a complete protein. This list includes buckwheat, hummus and pita, tofu, tempeh, edamame beans (soy), roasted and salted pumpkin seeds, peanut butter and toast, hemp, beans and rice, chia seeds, Ezekiel bread, quinoa, and spirulina.

Herbs

An herb is a plant with leaves, seeds, or flowers used for medicine, food, or flavoring. Herbs are used worldwide and can serve as a medical option (33). Natural medicines work with the skin, the heart, nervous, immune, circulatory, respiratory, endocrine, digestive, urinary, and musculoskeletal systems. A complete nutritional assessment is needed. Depending on you and your holistic practitioner, you can consume herbs in tea, pills, or a liquid applied to the skin or through the nasal passages. Remember to always seek out a trained expert in the field before beginning an herbal treatment protocol. Using herbs, in general, promotes balanced nutrition.

Herbs are used as medicine, treating many conditions.

Herbal treatment supports the cardiovascular system (blood vessels, heart, circulation, lymph nodes); the tissues (hair, bone, skin, joints, and muscle); the endocrine system, nervous system, and urinary tract (brain, thymus, pancreas, kidneys, bladder, adrenal glands, and central nervous system); and the digestive system and respiratory tract (liver, gallbladder, lungs, stomach, intestines, ears, eyes, and mouth). (33)

According to Andrew Chevallier, these herbs treat anxiety and depression. Author of the Encyclopedia of Herbal Medicine, (19) is a fellow of the National Institute of Medical Herbalists. He lists lemon balm, skullcap, damiana, valerian, ginseng, ashwagandha, St John's wort, lavender, chamomile flower, and kava kava. In addition, gokshura, shankhapushi, and Brahmi are included in the list given in The Way of Ayurvedic Herbs. (27)

Herbs to treat insomnia include chamomile, linden, lavender, hops, and passionflower. (19) Ashwagandha, tagara, nutmeg, and poppy seeds are also on the list. (27)

Foods and flavoring that boost health include carob and cinnamon. To address fibroids, menstrual issues, indigestion, liver cancer, and peptic ulcers, you can take coriander, cumin, dill, fennel, hemp, parsley, or thyme. (20)

Raw vs. cooked vegan foods

Raw vegetables are unprocessed vegetables that have not been heated over 104–118 degrees Fahrenheit (experts disagree about the temperature). Eating vegetables raw helps to maintain their enzymes and enhances their nutritional value, which helps restore the intestinal wall. In addition, consuming raw vegetables and other foods increases the amount of fiber intake.

The raw category includes all raw fruits/vegetables, nuts, seeds (soaked), sprouts, root vegetables and squashes, herbs and spices, and seaweeds. Raw foods can be dehydrated, juiced, blended, soaked, or sprouted. Research indicates that eating raw vegetables can reduce the risk of diabetes, help with weight loss, maintain a healthy weight for body configuration, and improve digestion. In addition, it provides optimal levels of folate and water-soluble vitamins. (28)

Cooked vegetables can soften the indigestible cellulose, releasing nutrients, which may not occur with raw vegetables (examples are carrots and tomatoes). In addition, the softened fibers of cooked vegetables release vitamins E and K and facilitate better mineral absorption.

Fruits

Boosting the immune system, fruits are a sweet and fleshy product of a tree or plant that contains a seed or seeds that can be consumed. (35) They are high in vitamins and minerals.

Fruits that support detoxification are apples, lemon, berries, pineapples, papaya, and pomegranate.

Fruits with the most nutrient density are white grapefruit, blackberries, pink or red grapefruit, limes, oranges, strawberries, and lemons. (30)

Alkaline fruits include avocado, persimmon, papayas,

lemons, limes, blueberries, plums, oranges, mangoes, grapes with seeds, apples, pears, pineapples, strawberries, peaches, kiwis, apricots, nectarines, honeydew cantaloupes, bananas, cherries, cooked tomatoes, and watermelons. (24)

Nuts (soaked and dehydrated)

All nuts should be soaked. There are different recommended times for soaking, but I practice something easy. I put my nuts in a bowl, rinse with water, and then keep them in fresh water overnight. I dehydrate them for hours if I want a different texture, like a crunchy taste.

Some recipes call for dehydration (nut mix), and sometimes I will only soak the nuts when making nut milk.

Benefits of soaking nuts:

1. Reduces mold. Nuts are stored for many years and can accumulate mold. This toxin produce mycotoxins, and soaking the nuts helps to reduce and eliminate the mold.
2. Nuts, especially those not organic, are sprayed with pesticides and chemicals. Cleaning the nuts will help to remove part of these chemicals.
3. Soaking nuts makes them more digestible, and the soaking process reduces phytic acid, lectins, and oxalates. These chemicals block the nutrient

compounds from being absorbed by the gut and aggravate the gut.

After soaking the nuts, you can consider dehydrating them, which will help to activate the nuts for better nutrition and absorption by the body. The water in the nuts is removed, making it easier on the digestive processes. As a result, the activated nuts will last longer. In addition, it will bring back a crunchy taste to the nuts.

Nutritious nuts to consider

Almonds improve cholesterol and reduce inflammation.

Pistachios are high in fiber, improve cholesterol, increase good HDL cholesterol, and improve blood pressure, weight loss, and oxidative status.

Walnuts contain omega-three fatty acids, improving health, lowering blood pressure, and increasing blood flow through the circulatory system.

Cashews are from the tree nut family, improve metabolic functioning and blood pressure, and provide antioxidants.

Pecans lower bad LDL cholesterol and provide antioxidants.

Macadamia nuts lower bad cholesterol and reduce heart disease factors.

Brazil nuts are a rich source of selenium, a mineral that acts as an antioxidant and can reduce inflammation. You only need a small amount for it to be effective.

Hazelnuts help reduce heart disease and cholesterol levels and increase the amount of vitamin E in the blood.

Peanuts are part of the legume family and are associated with lowering rates of diabetes and death and with improving heart disease risk. (18 & 30)

Adding all these nutrient-rich foods is beneficial. However, many other foods are not as helpful and should be cut back or eliminated. This list includes processed sugar, sodium, fat, dairy, and meat.

Cut back sugar

- Eating processed sugars and sodas can lead to addictive patterns. With little nutritional value, sugar is also high in calories.

  Foods high in sugar, sodium, and fat are related to obesity, heart disease, high blood pressure, and diabetes. Processed foods are stripped of most nutrients. The average American child consumes five pounds of sugar a week. (32) This includes starches, sugars, hydrogenated oils, artificial food dyes, flavoring, and salts. Most of these foods have had irradiation used on them, which is a process in which radiation eliminates mold, bacteria, and viruses, causing foods to lose their nutritional value. Sugar is an addictive substance and is often used as a sedative.

- Sugar promotes obesity and tooth decay, and certain cancers. (26) Try organic honey, maple syrup, or stevia during the transition period.
- Consumption of sugar and processed foods can cause disease. We are born with health. But by adding animal and processed foods to our bodies, we can damage the body and our health.
Eating those foods can cause DNA damage. As damaged cells are replicated, degenerative diseases advance and can lead to death. Processed food and sugar consumption are linked to an increased risk of cancer, celiac disease, and multiple sclerosis.
- Sugar is highly addictive (29) and linked to a higher risk of depression, mild cognitive impairment, anxiety (all of which are treated with pharmaceutical drugs), and ADHD. It can also lead to inflammation in the body and brain.
- Since sugar is quicker to digest, less energy is used, leading to weight gain. In processed foods, artificial ingredients are added, which can cause health problems. (30) Before you start to take things away, you must build up your body to succeed. Use fats, oils, and sweets sparingly.

HEAL THY MIND

Avoid dairy and meat

Besides cutting back sugar, you may also want to consider eliminating dairy and meat.

1. Dairy is a saturated fat associated with heart disease, type 2 diabetes, Alzheimer's, and acne. It can increase cholesterol and increase the risk for breast, ovarian, and prostate cancers (21 & 22) and Parkinson's disease (25).
2. Dairy is full of antibiotics. However, as cows develop antibiotic-resistant bacteria, antibiotics are less effective.
3. Dairy products such as casein contain casomorphins, a morphine-like compound. (23) When consumed, casomorphins attach to the same brain receptors as heroin. Casomorphins cause brain damage and effects like "morphine to the brain," mimicking psychosis. The inflammation in the brain can lead to irritability, anxiety, depression, and brain fog. (31)
4. Dairy is filled with sodium, contributing to heart disease.
5. Calcium in dairy is linked to weakened bones.
6. Hormones can increase estrogen levels.
7. Dairy can cause acid reflux symptoms. This is because humans lack the enzyme in the gut that is needed to break down the dairy. (31)

Besides dairy, meat is another food to avoid as you endeavor to improve your health.

Avoid Meat

Eating meat increases the risk for heart disease, diabetes, pneumonia, and bowel cancer. Meat consumption has also been associated with higher mortality, cardiovascular disease, colorectal cancer, and type 2 diabetes. (17) In addition, meat is filled with hormones and antibiotics. There are many political, nutritional, and spiritual problems around eating meat. (31) However, meat is associated with illness, and one should start now to move away from meat and towards vegetables.

Water is vital to good health!

Removing meat and dairy is vital to health. Along these lines, keeping your water consumption up is also essential! Water hydrates the body, helps the cells to be oxygenated, and removes toxic impurities. Options include coconut water, mineral water, spring water, glacier water, and alkaline water; water can be sparkling, distilled, purified, flavored, infused. Drink water as your primary liquid.

If you are not drinking enough water, your body will let you know with signs of dehydration. These can include dry skin, visible mucous membranes, headache, dark-colored urine, decreased urine output, nausea, vomiting, excessive thirst, dizziness, sluggishness, fatigue, weakness, dry mouth, swollen tongue, sugar cravings, confusion, heart palpitations, and bad breath. If you notice these symptoms, take measures to get rehydrated.

Supplements

Increasing water intake and taking supplements can enhance your health. I take many supplements for overall wellness and optimal health. I have done many things to determine a regime for myself based on diet, exercise, and detoxication. I have had urine, blood, hair, and stool samples tested over a few years. I know my food allergies and sensitivities as well. I know my blood and nutrient levels and get annual check-ups. I have done parasite cleanses, colonics, heavy metal detoxes, and fasting. You need to work with experts in the field to help get this part right and remain in balance. Levels and dosages of supplements change with underlying concerns and immune imbalances.

People have many fears about COVID. Debates about

HEAL THY MIND

vaccines and mandates across the world have dominated the headlines. I practice a supplement protocol to help build and support a healthy immune system. My protocol is listed below.

I have raw wheatgrass juice (Kamut) with glutathione and/or warm water with lemon in the morning. This is followed by black seed oil a few minutes later. Over the day, I ingest vitamins B, C, D, E, K1, and K2, calcium, quercetin, coenzyme Q, selenium, zinc sulfate, magnesium, potassium, astralagus, curcumin, melatonin, chlorella, probiotic (sometimes a prebiotic), and multivitamin and mineral supplements. I have found these supplements to move me towards optimal physical health. What supplements and dosages are needed for you depends on your current health. You can build your health naturally and holistically, and an expert in this field can serve as a guide in your plan towards healing. We must work to change our thoughts learned from our early years in school. Instead of focusing on meat and dairy, the food pyramid should focus on green vegetables, sprouts, grains, legumes, non-acid-forming nuts, seeds (soaked), sweet fruits and juices, and vitamins and minerals supplements. When you have moved toward consuming more vegetables, fruits, and seeds while avoiding processed foods and meats, you will be working towards wellness.

Another key to wellness, happiness, and success is exercising, which will be explored in the next chapter. of Exercise: Physical Health.

HEAL THY MIND

Takeaways

Nutrition is essential to healing the mind, but often challenging for most to change as it reveals traumatic and attachment patterns of suffering and pain. The body must heal itself so the mind can heal. You can't heal the mind without working on the physical body. Spend the time and energy to work with a professional, because your body has specific needs. Learn and understand what the body needs to sustain alkalinity, as this supports optimal health. Consider natural and organic ways to heal the body. There are fewer side effects than relying on prescribed or over-the-counter medications. Invest in herbs and supplements that repair, replenish, and restore the body.

HEAL THY MIND

Self-reflections

1. Reflect on your diet. What does it say about you?
2. Note simple ways to incorporate more vegetables and herbs into your diet.
3. Write down a supplement plan for the morning, afternoon, and evening routines.
4. What dairy, meat, processed foods, or sugary items are you giving up this month?
5. What new recipes will you try to include using raw vegetables this month?
6. Write a list of your symptoms and explore natural ways to heal the body.
7. How will you communicate the new eating changes to friends and family? How will you plan for holidays, vacations, celebrations, and outdoor events?

6

EXERCISE: PHYSICAL HEALTH

Proverb: No time for health today, no health for your time tomorrow. (Irish proverb)

Affirmation: I move my body; I sustain my health; I am physical.

HEAL THY MIND

If clients like to play basketball, we shoot hoops in the exercise room. If playing with Nerf guns is their thing, we play as we process trauma in the body. If they like crafting, we paint, color, or create. If they like Legos, we build until their heart is content. But, before we delve deeper into their challenges, I like to get the blood pumping, providing opportunities for the body to release trauma, especially with children and teens.

Moving your body is just as important as the other items with the OCTAVES method. When we are young, we participate in school activities and walk to places such as school or the park. We get out, moving our bodies over the course of our days. As we age, these activities decline for most people. The goal is to boost your activity level, not compare yourself to others.

What I do for my physical health in terms of intensity and frequency will differ from what other people do. When deciding where to start with an exercise routine, you want to include something that improves your heart rate with cardio exercises. You want to sweat. It helps with the detoxing process through the skin, purifying your internal organs, and increases blood flow in the body. You will develop stronger lungs as you work on breath control with cardio. The second part is to do some strength training exercises. This builds your muscle mass, which decreases with age, and supports stronger bones, reducing your risk for fractures.

Importance of exercise

Exercise improves high blood pressure. It decreases stress and the risk for diabetes and heart disease. It improves sleep, though it is not recommended to engage in cardio 3–5 hours before bedtime. It improves and/or stabilizes cognition, anxiety, depression, and other trauma-induced symptoms. For your mental health, exercise releases feel-good endorphins (the brain's natural chemical to enhance your overall good feelings). It moves your thoughts away from the negativity often associated with depression and anxiety. The more consistently you exercise, the more confident you feel; your social interactions increase, and you feel more actively involved in your health. As a result, you take control of your physical health and mental health. (36)

Walk your way out of anxiety

There was a period during the COVID pandemic when we were all in the house. I walked three to five times a day before, during, and after seeing patients remotely. My schedule was exhausting, and I had a plan going into the next several months. I did everything in the OCTAVES method, but I walked, walked, and walked more. My stress was managed—no anxiety and no negative thoughts constantly forming, occupying space in my mind. I felt great (my dogs were tired and hid from me at times), and walking was helping.

Change with the season

Like your diet, your exercise routine should change with the season. Of course, this is different depending on where you live. Below is a list of suggested activities for each season, keeping in mind that you want your exercise to align with the season and nature.

Spring is a time when most people see more sunlight. They enjoy the cool breeze with increased temperatures, fresh flowers, birds chatting, and new babies being born. Spring is about renewals, regrowth, and rejuvenation.
  Cardio: gardening, running (intermittent), hiking, softball, cycling, horseback riding. People tend to feel more motivated in preparation for summer. This is a time to keep your motivation high.
  Strength training: use machines at a local park, watch videos, walk with leg/arm weights, or join a group class.

Summer is usually the warmest part of the year. However, it

can be hot and dry, depending on where you live. This is a period of fulfillment, happiness, and beauty.

Cardio: swimming, tennis, volleyball, dancing, kayaking, and sailing.

Strength training: lifting weights (faster and harder), going to the gym or workout class, and stretching (holding longer and deeper).

Fall brings new changes. Things are cooling down in the transition to fall, plants become dormant (resting), and the natural world changes or brightens in color. As your exercise changes, you may need to increase your organic healthy foods.

Cardio: kickboxing, attending fall festivals for walking, preparing for cross country (run longer but steady), going out for shopping needs (no home delivery), football, ice hockey, and lacrosse.

Strength training: deep stretching class, weight training (more repetitions and less weight), home routines (three times per day), and inverted poses (headstands, cartwheels).

Winter is usually the coldest season. In the air, there is frost and snow. The rain spreads its magic. There is also an increase in depression during this time. In preparation, we must work harder to be physically active. This is a time to review your physical goals, ensuring you are on track for the upcoming months.

Cardio: learn to ski, snowboard, or mountain climb in the snow, build a snowman and have a snowball fight, use your indoor equipment (bike, treadmill) more frequently, do your home routines in the heat to help sweat, go to ice- and roller-skating rinks, or go for group walks indoors (e.g., in the mall or department stores).

Strength training: plan workout parties or active games to play (e.g., for every wrong answer, people must sit on the wall), go to a local indoor gym, and use resistance bands, kettlebells, or dumbbells. Implement stretching (shorter time holding posture and then go fast).

Keep in mind that you may still engage in the same activities but change the intensity and frequency.

I did not mention yoga in this section. This is because yoga has been mistranslated to be a form of exercise in the United States and other countries. I do not mention yoga here, because for me, yoga is not a physical activity but a spiritual one. Therefore, you can think of traditional yoga classes as exercise practice, group social period, workout, etc.

HEAL THY MIND

Exercise for trauma survivors

I want to clarify. I am highly skilled in teaching patients to work on trauma using adjunctive practices. One such practice is trauma-sensitive yoga. I want to explain that this is a treatment option, not a form of exercise. For example, you will experience various sensations in your body in the process. You may sweat or experience changes in breathing patterns, and you will often feel an emotional release. This is part of the "t" in trauma. It is recommended for trauma survivors to move their bodies. Symptoms associated with trauma decrease with the body's physical movement. (37) As you do cardio, you begin to control the fluctuations in your heart rate. As you implement strength training, you begin to choose how, why, when, and where to move and strengthen your body.

It is an option for you to make decisions about your physical health. Here are some questions to get started.

A. What exercise/movement/attention does your body need every day?
B. Cardio is essential for everyone. What cardio regime do you want to start with?
C. Strength training is essential for everyone. What practices are you open to exploring?
D. What physical changes are needed to improve your sleep and eating habits?

HEAL THY MIND

E. I encourage all my patients to watch less TV and be more active. What choices have you made to increase your activity all day?

F. Take notice of what sensations arise in your body with your physical health and explore them in therapy with your trauma clinician.

Recommendations

I want all my patients, friends, family, and the whole world to watch less TV and be more active. Make choices to increase your activity all day. Take notice of what sensations arise in your body regarding your physical health as you exercise and explore them in therapy with your trauma clinician. Adding more exercise will enhance your health.

HEAL THY MIND

Takeaways

Move your body throughout the day every day. Build up your energy and fight fatigue. However, if you are experiencing fatigue (mental or physical), seek to understand the underlying issue and address it. Fatigue is the first sign of illness. You don't have to wait for a blood test or a medical doctor to tell you. If you are fatigued during the day, then you are moving towards a diseased state. Exercise is essential to prevent disease. Listen to your body and your mind. Staying active over the year doing various exercises will keep you energized. Change with nature to stay in balance. Remember, if you are working on trauma, this does not excuse you from doing your exercise; it gives you the freedom to choose what exercises and what movements you choose to do with your body. Adding more exercise will enhance your health. And socializing will also benefit you in your journey to wellness. Socializing will be the final part of the OCTAVES method, learning to accept yourself and build relationships with others.

HEAL THY MIND

Self-reflections

1. Explore what activities you will consider for fall, winter, spring, and summer.
2. Reflect on and write down daily cardio and strength training goals.
3. Note any sensations in your body when physically active.
4. Explore how you can include more physical activity during the day.
5. What tools, apps, or technologies can you use to motivate yourself? You may also consider changing this with the seasons as well. In the fall, I use my Apple watch to count steps (10,000 steps is my daily goal). In the winter, I use it to count calories burned. In the spring, I walk more frequently, which is how I measure my exercise. I have a rigid training protocol and diet in the summer, so this is my measure.
6. What seasons or months are most difficult for you? Write down a plan to be physically active 3–6 months prior.
7. When you were a child, what goals and thoughts did you have about your physical body? What were your fantasies, dreams, and desires?

7

SOCIALIZE: RELATIONSHIP HEALTH

Proverb: People are often unreasonable, irrational, and self-centered. Forgive them anyway. If you are kind, people may accuse you of selfish, ulterior motives. Be kind anyway. If you are successful, you will win some unfaithful friends and some genuine enemies. Succeed anyway. If you are honest and sincere people may deceive you. Be honest and sincere anyway. What you spend years creating, others could destroy overnight. Create anyway. If you find serenity and happiness, some may be jealous. Be happy anyway. The good you do today will often be forgotten. Do good anyway. Give the best you have, and it will never be enough. Give your best anyway. In the final analysis, it is between you and God. It was never between you and them. (Mother Theresa saying)

Affirmation: I am accepting of myself.

I care for me; so I can care 4 u

No one is born wise about relationships. However, we have experiences that help us understand more about ourselves over our lifetimes. We have parents to guide us, who give us opportunities to learn lessons and learn about ourselves. Children also provide us with opportunities to grow. The emotional attachment in these relationships can be intense. For example, there is an assumption that we should love our biological children. Yet, this can lead you towards disappointment, unresolved anger, and frustrations. We tend to focus more on the other person, what they did or did not do. Kids become the problem, or our parents become the problem. If a relationship is emotionally abusive, we assume it is not healthy. We need to reframe our thinking about relationships. Healthy relationships start from within you. As you reflect, you can open a space of balance, appreciating

HEAL THY MIND

all life's experiences. These are opportunities for us to focus on ourselves.

We all have "good" and "bad" stuff. You can work to understand what makes you tick and what triggers you. To do this, you need support from someone who is clinically and spiritually trained, to help navigate the ego. The ego will trick you. The ego knows you better than anyone or anything. It knows your deepest unconscious fears, worries, anxieties, attractions, and desires. The ego will trick you in this process. As you begin to understand the good and bad things in yourself, you can go deeper. You can choose the stuff you want to keep, the stuff you want to change, and the stuff you want to destroy.

Humility is a quality that allows one to rise above and beyond these lower and negative parts of the ego. For example, some people seek money, fame, possessions, and beauty and still feel lonely, unloved, or not good enough, so they may not have the answer to happiness. Someone may desire a husband or wife. Once they get married, they have a desire for children. Then they wish for the children to leave. Others may want a job, then a promotion, then another promotion. If one continues to feed into this cycle, it becomes imprinted into the mind, into one's thoughts, feelings, behaviors, and reactions. The result can contribute to illness and disease. Humility gives you a space to operate with a higher level of authenticity. You desire deeper, more meaningful, and more honorable things in this life. It brings you closer to being God-like, which is your true nature. For me, buying a house or car became less significant, and being true to my virtues in my relationships with myself and others brought me a feeling of bliss and genuine happiness.

Are you practicing humility?

The solution to interpersonal relationships lies within you. People struggle with relationships, because there are distortions.

These distortions fall into several categories.

1. *Catastrophic thinking* is when the person always focuses on the worst outcome. For example, if a child doesn't call by a specific time, the parent assumes they have been in an accident.
2. *Personalization* is where the person focuses everything on themselves. For example, someone at the store is waiting in line. Someone else bumps into them. The first person assumes the second person did it on purpose.

3. *Jumping to conclusions* is where a person believes falsehoods or accusations. For example, when a girlfriend is late, you think she wants to break up with you.

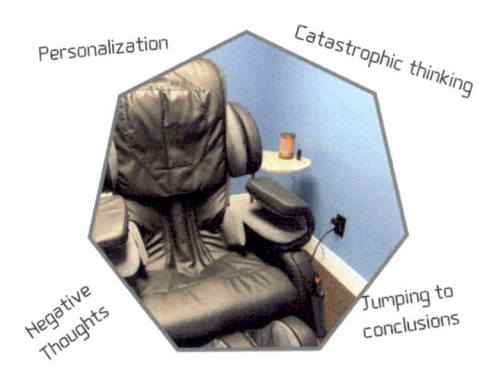

Negative thinking patterns make relationships difficult. You need to know your cognitive distortions; it helps you understand yourself. (Leu, L., 2015). Most therapy treatments stop with cognitive distortions. I go deeper, finding out the root of the cognitive distortion. For example, if a mom feels her daughter is irritable, then she makes assumptions. "My daughter never wants to talk to me. She stays in her room. She must hate me. I am a bad parent." The mom must understand the distortions, what is being revealed about her. Discovering the good and the bad is therapeutic. When patients feel safe with the clinician, they will slowly reveal more. Figuring out triggers, what makes you react, can be helpful.

A trigger is a memory—unconscious, conscious, or

epigenetic—of an experience or event or something the mind perceives as something else. Triggers can be about past relationships (including issues of trust and mistrust and unresolved other problems), current behaviors of other people, fears, phobias, curiosity or lack of curiosity, or social and emotional isolation. You can also be triggered if you have experienced disappointment or resentment, lack of boundaries, or forced boundaries. Through deep reflection, the person must identify the good and bad stuff in their life to move towards wellness, happiness, and success. It is beneficial to collaborate with a trained professional in this process.

Where are your triggers stored?

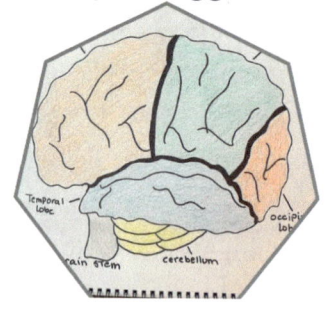

By setting aside distortions, you can move towards healthy relationships. It is within you. You can learn to appreciate life and others around you. You start with yourself, because the solutions reside within the individual. Here are seven reasons to start with yourself in building relationships.

1. Real change starts from within.
2. It improves one's health.
3. If you are healthy, other people around you will change.
4. You get to know yourself better.
5. It brings balance.
6. Starting with yourself builds confidence and dynamic self-esteem.
7. It helps you know a healthy lifestyle and practice healthy relationships. (38)

We are familiar with what an unhealthy relationship looks like because of our interaction. Yet, most of us think a healthy relationship is the opposite of prior relationships. This is partly true. For example, an emotionally abusive relationship is unhealthy; therefore the assumption is that if there is no abuse, then this is a healthy relationship. However, a healthy relationship is when you understand, accept, and appreciate yourself. You are in balance, and this is a healthy relationship. You will no longer tolerate mistreatment, be disturbed, or negatively influence others. A healthy relationship is within and not external. These are some signs that you are moving towards wellness.

- You set aside time for self-reflection and meditation.
- You show compassion and forgiveness for yourself.
- You engage in therapeutic processes and guidance.

HEAL THY MIND

- You smile and laugh a lot.
- You care about the foods and liquids you put into your body.
- You move your body frequently and try new, active things.
- You love everyone. You forgive everyone. You show compassion to everyone. (38) Remember that socializing and building relationships is a process you are moving towards. However, there are hiccups in life. It is crucial to get back on track when these occur and accept yourself.
-

Here are some ideas to improve relationship health in your life.

1. Spend time alone.
2. Engage in physical activity.
3. Go to see a movie alone, without a phone.
4. Start a new hobby.
5. Write a letter or make a video to your younger self or older self.
6. Listen to music or go to see plays that are different rather than familiar.
7. Travel and try new things to discover who you are.

HEAL THY MIND

Takeaways

Do you have a healthy relationship with yourself?

Understand and accept the "good" and "bad," because this is what makes you perfect. We all need to work on this balance. This is where humility comes into place. Remember, the work is with you, and your first social relationship in life was with yourself, and then your primary caregivers. Start there and develop a relationship with yourself that brings about healing, wellness, happiness, and success. Only you can discover this. Along the way, many people can be your guides in this process.

Self-reflections

1. What makes a true friend?
2. What do you give away, and what do you gain in relationships with others?
3. What have you learned about yourself in relationships with others?
4. Who are you in relation to your assigned roles in life?
5. What can you do to support deeper, intimate relationships with others?
6. What triggers you in relationships, and what does this say about the type of work you need to do?
7. What is a healthy relationship for you, and how can you find environments and experiences that support your engagement in these relationships?

NEXT STEPS:
A GUIDE TO A HEALTHY LIFE

My journey with the OCTAVES method

As a child, I was born into a world where I felt loved, nurtured, and encouraged. I was given affection, attention, and admiration. Life then began to happen. In my early teens, I struggled with peer relationships and struggled to fit in most of the time. I struggled academically because of an undiagnosed learning disorder. In sixth grade, I felt abandoned by my father, and things started to change for me. I was popular, a mediocre athlete, and socially connected yet mentally disconnected from my peers in adolescence. However, I lived in a violent, crime-infested area, so feeling safe was difficult. I had moments of being neglected, abused, and unheard, making my voice stay silent. Continuing my path of not believing in myself, I didn't think I was good enough.

My twenties were the most challenging time for me. I hit a form of depression that made life seem unbearable most of the time. I struggled to understand my role in intimate and family relationships, not knowing my worth. I struggled with my son's father, because we were always fighting. My first connection with therapy was when I participated in counseling while attending UCI. I worked with an older lady, a motherly figure, who helped me sort out my feelings and thoughts about myself. I was permitted to leave relationships that were not good for me. I was given permission to work on me. It seemed simple. Until this day, our work still impacts me in a meaningful way. I also started meditation and worship practices. Deciding to become vegetarian, I became physically fit and active as well. So, you see, I had already started with some preparation of the OCTAVES method, but things were not all in place. During that time, I was still suffering.

In my thirties, stressors increased, and the challenges of being a college student, working several jobs, being a single parent, and living alone brought both complications and joys. I was anxious on most days. I tried psychotropic medications. I ate unhealthy foods and ate a lot. It was not until my late thirties and early forties that my mental struggles with childhood traumas, depression, and anxiety were addressed and managed.

This was when I was ready to be more active in my mental health and discover ways to heal my mind. As I learned to cure myself—because we all have the cure deep within us—a light flickered on for me. I found a spiritual reconnection—my reconnection back with God and a community congruent with my beliefs. This was when the OCTAVES method began to manifest deeply in a meaningful and authentic way.

O—Observation: My practice is intentional and consistent. I mediate both informally and formally. I have found my spiritual path, and it brings a sense of relief and connection. I have found my home. I discovered this in my twenties, but I lost the path, and now I have found the reconnection.

C—Compassion: I work on showing compassion and forgiveness to all things, people, events, etc. I send myself reminders and encourage family, particularly my children and mom, who remind me consistently to demonstrate compassion through their behaviors.

T—Therapy: I have found two clinicians in my therapy journey who have helped me understand more about myself. Although painful and challenging at times, the process still benefits me. Then I engage with therapeutic supports and activities, both formal and informal. This includes taking courses, journaling, reading, listening, sitting in silence, etc. My religion is therapeutic and serves as a guide and a way of being based on truth, justice, righteousness, reciprocity, balance, order, and harmony.

A—Animals: I learned to appreciate animals and all living things. I have worked on phobias, discomforts, and mental challenges regarding insects, rodents, and wild animals. I am playful and goofy, and I laugh a lot. I get many opportunities to be creative and expressive, experiencing many childlike moments in my life.

V—Victuals: I am vegan and transitioning towards raw veganism. I have removed meat and dairy from my diet. In addition, I am working to remove sugars, starches, and processed foods. This involves a different mental strength, preparation, and detaching myself from things, events, memories, beliefs, etc.

E—Exercise: I have tried many different sports. Some I have enjoyed, and some I don't practice. I spend more time in nature. I appreciate the sun, the moon, and the stars. I move my body in group classes and home routines. I encourage my friends and family to move more and eat less.

S—Socialize: I have professional and leisure relationships. I have superficial conversations with various people and more profound, meaningful relationships with those closest to me. I love all people and work not to fear anyone.

Practice, practice, and practice again. This should become a regular part of your routine as you work towards a mental wellness plan. There will be hiccups. Be compassionate and forgiving towards yourself and get back on your mental wellness plan. There will be negative thoughts, and although familiar, this is where the work starts. These thoughts are helpful and can be sorted out in therapy as you keep moving forward. Please don't ignore the thoughts; let them be a teacher. As you come to understand these thoughts, consider if you want to make a change. There will be people who will sabotage your process. Remember that it is not about them but about your own vulnerability and fears about reaching your mental wellness, happiness, and success. You can be healthy. You can achieve happiness. You can achieve success. You can change. You can heal. Here is a guide to help you develop your mental wellness plan using the OCTAVES method.

Observation

- Attend a spiritual or religious activity alone or with a friend.
- Engage in different forms of meditation.
- Stay and sit in silence or go on a silent retreat.

Compassion

- Show compassion all the time to everyone, including yourself.
- Do nice things for those close to you weekly.
- Make meaningful and sentimental gifts for others.

Therapy

- Be willing to pay for your treatment.
- Do your homework and commit (at least 1.5–2 years to start).
- Write down your goals for therapy.

Animals

- Have fun and laugh.
- Appreciate all living things and creatures.
- Spend time in nature outdoors.

Victuals

- Eat vegetables, herbs, and fruits daily.
- Prepare most meals at home.
- Eat one meal a week outdoors to connect with nature.

HEAL THY MIND

Exercise

- Move your body in the morning, afternoon, and evening.
- Try a new exercise/sport one to four times per year.
- Go to a national or local park once per year.

Socialize

- Have a conversation with someone different from you once per month.
- Start a journal (audio, visual, or written).
- Plan a vacation by yourself.

HEAL THY MIND

Using all these tools from the OCTAVES methods, you can heal and live a healthy life! Understand and accept the "good" and "bad," because this is what makes you perfect. We all need to work on this balance. This is where humility comes into place. Remember, the work is with you, and your first social relationship in life was with yourself, and then your primary caregivers. So, start there and develop a relationship with yourself that brings about healing, wellness, happiness, and success. Only you can discover this. Many people can guide you in this process.

Heal Thy Mind: Seven Strategies Towards Wellness, Happiness, and Success is a practical guide to use. These seven strategies are designed to be integrative. Work on devising a plan including all these elements to achieve your mental wellness. In my many years of doing this work, I have healed one person, myself. However, I have been the guide and consulted with thousands of people. You have the capability to heal. Remember, you have one goal in life: to work on yourself. This guide will move you in the direction of health and wellness.

If you are searching for a clinician or need tips on moving toward health and wellness, I would be excited to assist you on your journey and would enjoy hearing from you. Here is my contact information if you would like to connect with me.

Tonya Octave, Licensed Clinical Social Worker (LCSW)

For more information, please visit:
https://tonyaoctave-lcsw.com/

Email: tonyaoctave-lcsw.com

Podcast: Trauma and Social Work

Instagram, Facebook, Twitter: HolisticClinician

For a free account with NES Bioenergetic Healing:
https://www.energy4life.com/p/tonyaoctave

You can review the recommended resources listed after the citation section to enhance your wellness knowledge. Please visit my website for an updated list of resources and subscribe to "Know Thyself: An Integrative Mental Wellness Hustle" monthly newsletter.

CITATIONS

Chapter 1 Observation

(1) Center for Trauma and Embodiment at JRI. (2020). *Trauma Center Trauma-Sensitive Yoga and Program of the Center for Trauma & Embodiment at JRI.* https://www.traumasensitiveyoga.com/

Chapter 2 Compassion

(2) ASA Authors & Reviewers. Sleep Physician at American Sleep Association Reviewers and Writers Board-certified sleep M.D. physicians, scientists, editors and writers for ASA. (2021, December 3). *American Sleep Association: Insomnia, Sleep Apnea & Snoring.* American Sleep Association. https://www.sleepassociation.org/

(3) *CDC - How Much Sleep Do I Need? - Sleep and Sleep Disorders.* (2021). Sleep and Sleep Disorders. https://www.cdc.gov/sleep/about_sleep/how_much_sleep.html

(4) Souders, B. M. (2021, December 6). *What is Forgiveness and What Are the Benefits?* PositivePsychology.Com. https://positivepsychology.com/forgiveness-benefits/

(5) *SpreadKindness.org.* (2021). Https://Www.Spreadkindness.Org/. https://www.spreadkindness.org/

(6) Troy, D. (2021, October 5). *Home Page.* Sleep Education. https://sleepeducation.org/

Chapter 3 Therapy

(7) *Association for Play Therapy: Mental Health Professionals Applying the Therapeutic Power of Play.* (2021). Https://Www.A4pt.Org/. https://www.a4pt.org/

(8) Emerson, D., & PhD, W. J. (2015). *Trauma-Sensitive Yoga in Therapy: Bringing the Body into Treatment* (Illustrated ed.). W. W. Norton & Company

(9) *Who We Are.* (2013, October 2). Http://Iarpp.Net/Who-We-Are/. http://iarpp.net/who-we-are/

(10) Hunt, J. R. (2021, November 2). *TF-CBT Certification Program - Official Website.* Trauma Focus Cognitive Behavioral Therapy Certification Program. https://tfcbt.org/

(11) Wilson-Lindberg, V. L. (2019, February 1). *Play Therapy: 5 Reasons Why It's So Effective*. The Guidance Center. https://www.tgclb.org/play-therapy/5-reasons-its-so-effective/

Chapter 4 Animals: Playful Inner Health

(12) A. (2020, November 4). *Parents' Guide to the Stages of Play*. Pathways.Org. https://pathways.org/watch/parents-guide-stages-play/

(13) A. (2021, December 3). *What Kind of Animals Can Be Emotional Support Animals?* Mango Clinic. https://mangoclinic.com/emotional-support-animals-types/

(14) Dogs, A. O. T. (2020, October 27). *Therapy Dog | Therapy Dog Organizations*. Alliance of Therapy Dogs Inc. https://www.therapydogs.com/

(15) Li, M. P. S. (2021, December 31). *Importance of Play in Early Childhood (9 Benefits & Infographic)*. Parenting For Brain. https://www.parentingforbrain.com/benefits-play-learning-activities-early-childhood/

(16) Robinson, L. (2021, December 9). *The Benefits of Play for Adults*. HelpGuide.Org. https://www.helpguide.org/articles/mental-health/benefits-of-play-for-adults.htm

Chapter 5 Victuals

(17) Battaglia Richi E, Baumer B, Conrad B, Darioli R, Schmid A, Keller U. Health Risks Associated with Meat Consumption: A Review of Epidemiological Studies, Int j Vitam Nutr Res. 2015;85(1-2): 70-8. doj: 10.1024/0300-9831/a000224. PMID: 26780279

(18) Bender, B., PhD. (2018, September 28). *Healthiest Nuts: 16 Nutritious Nuts Ranked from Best to Worst*. Intake Health. https://www.intake.health/post/healthiest-nuts-16-nutritious-nuts-ranked-from-best-to-worst

(19) Chevallier, A. (2016). *Encyclopedia of Herbal Medicine: 550 Herbs and Remedies for Common Ailments* (3rd edition). DK.

(20) Cnc, P. B. A., & Bell, S. (2012). *Prescription for Herbal Healing, 2nd Edition: An Easy-to-Use A-to-Z Reference to Hundreds of Common Disorders and Their Herbal Remedies* (Updated ed.). Avery.

(21) Dagfinn Aune, Deborah A Navarro Rosenblatt, Doris SM Chan, Ana Rita Vieira, Rui Vieira, Darren C Greenwood, Lars J Vatten, Teresa Norat, Dairy products, calcium, and prostate cancer risk: a systematic review and meta-analysis of cohort studies, *The American Journal of Clinical Nutrition*, Volume 101, Issue 1, January 2015, Pages 87-117m https://doi.org/10.3945/ajcn.113.067157

(22) Greenwood, Lars J Vatten, Teresa Norat, Dairy products, calcium, and prostate cancer risk: A systematic review and meta-analysis of cohort studies, *The American Journal of Clinical Nutrition*, Volume 101, Issue 1, January 2015, Pages 87–117, https://doi.org/10.3945/ajcn.113.067157

(23) Duc Doan Nguyen, Stuart Keith Johnson, Francesco Busetti & Vicky Ann Solah (2015) Formation and Degradation of Beta-casomorphins in Dairy Processing, Critical Reviews in Food Science and Nutrition, 55:14, 1955-1967, DOI: 10.1080/10408398.2012.740102

(24) Henele, D. (2022). *Energetic Health: Interesting Insights Into Advanced Natural Medicine (Volume 1) by Dr Henele (2013–10-01)* (3rd ed., Vol. 1). CreateSpace Independent Publishing Platform; 3rd Edition (2013–10-01).

(25) Hughes, K. C., Gao, X., Kim, I. Y., Wang, M., Weisskopf, M. G., Schwarzschild, M. A., & Ascherio, A. (2017). Intake of dairy foods and risk of Parkinson disease. *Neurology, 89*(1), 46–52. https://doi.org/10.1212/WNL.0000000000004057

(26) Janjua, H. U. (2016, February 2). *Effects of sugar, salt and distilled water on white blood cells and platelet cells: A review | Janjua | Journal of Tumor*. Journal Of Tumor. http://www.ghrnet.org/index.php/JT/article/view/1340/1795

(27) Khalsa, K. P. S., & Tierra, M. (2008). *The Way of Ayurvedic Herbs* (1st ed.). Lotus Press.

(28) McNish, D. (2012). *Eat Raw, Eat Well: 400 Raw, Vegan and Gluten-Free Recipes*. Robert Rose.

(29) Maffetone, P. (2020, March 24). *SPECIAL REPORT: Sugar is a Drug*. Dr. Phil Maffetone. https://philmaffetone.com/special-report-sugar-is-a-drug/

(30) Mateljan, G. (2006). *The World's Healthiest Foods: Essential Guide for the Healthiest Way of Eating* (1st ed.). GMF Publishing.

(31) Robbins, J. (2012). *Diet for a New America: How Your Food Choices Affect Your Health, Happiness, and the Future of Life on Earth Second Edition* (25th Anniversary ed.). HJ Kramer/New World Library.

(32) The Diabetes Council. (2018, July 10). *45 Alarming Statistics on American's Sugar Consumption and the Effects of Sugar on Americans' Health.* TheDiabetesCouncil.Com. https://www.thediabetescouncil.com/45-alarming-statistics-on-americans-sugar-consumption-and-the-effects-of-sugar-on-americans-health/

(33) Wikipedia contributors. (2021a, December 14). *Herb.* Https://En.Wikipedia.Org/Wiki/Herb. https://en.wikipedia.org/wiki/Herb

(34) Wikipedia contributors. (2021b, December 27). *Vegetable.* Https://En.Wikipedia.Org/Wiki/Vegetable. https://en.wikipedia.org/wiki/Vegetable

(35) Wikipedia contributors. (2022, January 1). *Fruit.* Https://En.Wikipedia.Org/Wiki/Fruit. https://en.wikipedia.org/wiki/Fruit

Chapter 6 Exercise

(36) Mikkelsen K, Stojanovska L, Polenakovic M, Bosevski M, Apostolopoulos V. Exercise and Mental Health. Maturitas. 2017 Dec; 106:48-56. doi: 10.1016/j.maturitas.2017.09.003. Epub 2017 Sep 7. PMID: 29150166.

(37) Emerson, D., & PhD, W. J. (2015). *Trauma-Sensitive Yoga in Therapy: Bringing the Body intoTreatment* (Illustrated ed.). W. W. Norton & Company.

Chapter 7 Socialization

(38) Leu, L. (2015). *NONVIOLENT COMMUNICATION : Companion Workbook - A Practical Guide for Individual, Group, or Classroom Study* (2nd ed.). Raj Publication.

For an updated list of resources, including a list of professionals in your area, please visit my website. https://tonyaoctave-lcsw.com/contact-me/

RECOMMENDED RESOURCES

Recommended for Observation

Ashby, M. (2011). *AFRICAN RELIGION Volume 4: ASARIAN THEOLOGY: RESURRECTING OSIRIS The path of Mystical Awakening and the Keys to Immortality*. Sema Institute.

Ashby, M. (2005). *Egyptian Yoga: The Philosophy of Enlightenment* (2nd ed.). Sema Institute.

Emerson, D., & PhD, W. J. (2015). *Trauma-Sensitive Yoga in Therapy: Bringing the Body into Treatment* (Illustrated ed.). W. W. Norton & Company.

Lama, D., Tutu, D., & Abrams, D. C. (2016). *The Book of Joy: Lasting Happiness in a Changing World* (Illustrated ed.). Avery.

Rama, S., Ballentine, MD, R., & Ajaya, PhD, S. (1976). *Yoga & Psychotherapy The Evolution of Consciousness*. Himalayan Institute India.

HEAL THY MIND

Recommended for Compassion

Brown, B. (2010). *The Gifts of Imperfection: Let Go of Who You Think You're Supposed to Be and Embrace Who You Are* (1st ed.). Hazelden Publishing.

Brown, T. (2021). *Feeding the Soul (Because It's My Business): Finding Our Way to Joy, Love, and Freedom*. William Morrow.

CDC - How Much Sleep Do I Need? - Sleep and Sleep Disorders. (2021). Sleep and Sleep Disorders. https://www.cdc.gov/sleep/about_sleep/how_much_sleep.html

Huffington, A. (2017). *The Sleep Revolution: Transforming Your Life, One Night at a Time* (Reprint ed.). Harmony.

M.D., C. D., & Ph.D., R. T. E. (2020). *The Healing Self: A Revolutionary New Plan to Supercharge Your Immunity and Stay Well for Life* (Illustrated ed.). Harmony.

Simon, D., MD, & Chopra, D. (2012). *The Wisdom of Healing*. Harmony/Rodale.

Sleep Physician at American Sleep Association Reviewers and Writers Board-certified sleep M.D. physicians, scientists, editors and writers for ASA. (2021, December 3). *American Sleep Association: Insomnia, Sleep Apnea & Snoring*. American Sleep Association. https://www.sleepassociation.org/

Souders, B. M. (2021, December 6). *What is Forgiveness and What Are the Benefits?* PositivePsychology.Com. https://positivepsychology.com/forgiveness-benefits/

SpreadKindness.org. (2021). Https://Www.Spreadkindness.Org/. https://www.spreadkindness.org/

Troy, D. (2021, October 5). *Home Page*. Sleep Education. https://sleepeducation.org/

Tutu, D., & Tutu, M. (2015). *The Book of Forgiving: The Fourfold Path for Healing Ourselves and Our World* (Illustrated ed.). Harper One.

Huffington, A. (2017). *The Sleep Revolution: Transforming Your Life, One Night at a Time* (Reprint ed.). Harmony.

Recommended for Therapy

Abram, B., Howard, M. A., & Stephens, M. (2018). *Teaching Trauma-Sensitive Yoga: A Practical Guide* (Illustrated ed.). North Atlantic Books.

Association for Play Therapy: Mental Health Professionals Applying the Therapeutic Power of Play. (2021). Https://Www.A4pt.Org/. https://www.a4pt.org/

Emerson, D., & PhD, W. J. (2015). *Trauma-Sensitive Yoga in Therapy: Bringing the Body into Treatment* (Illustrated ed.). W. W. Norton & Company.

Hunt, J. R. (2021, November 2). *TF-CBT Certification Program - Official Website*. Trauma Focus Cognitive Behavioral Therapy Certification Program. https://tfcbt.org/

Lipsky, V. L. D., & Burk, C. (2009). *Trauma Stewardship: An Everyday Guide to Caring for Self While Caring for Others* (1st ed.). Berrett-Koehler Publishers.

Menakem, R. (2017). *My Grandmother's Hands: Racialized Trauma and the Pathway to Mending Our Hearts and Bodies* (Illustrated ed.). Central Recovery Press.

Van Der Kolk, M.D., B. (2014). *The Body Keeps the Score: Brain, Mind, and Body in the Healing of Trauma*. Penguin Group (USC) LLC.

Wachtel, P. L. (2010). *Relational Theory and the Practice of Psychotherapy* (1st ed.). The Guilford Press.

Who We Are. (2013, October 2). Http://Iarpp.Net/Who-We-Are/. http://iarpp.net/who-we-are/

Wiener, J., & Rosen, D. H. (2017). *The Therapeutic Relationship: Transference, Countertransference, and the Making of Meaning (Volume 14) (Carolyn and Ernest Fay Series in Analytical Psychology)* (Reprint ed.). Texas A&M University Press.

Wilson-Lindberg, V. L. (2019, February 1). *Play Therapy: 5 Reasons Why It's So Effective*. The Guidance Center.

Recommended for Animals: Playful Inner Health

A. (2020, November 4). *Parents' Guide to the Stages of Play.* Pathways.Org. https://pathways.org/watch/parents-guide-stages-play/

A. (2021, December 3). *What Kind of Animals Can Be Emotional Support Animals?* Mango Clinic. https://mangoclinic.com/emotional-support-animals-types/

Dogs, A. O. T. (2020, October 27). *Therapy Dog | Therapy Dog Organizations.* Alliance of Therapy Dogs Inc. https://www.therapydogs.com/

Elliott, R. (2014). *The Big Book of Laugh-Out-Loud Jokes for Kids.* Van Haren Publishing.

Estes, C. P. (2008). *(Women Who Run with the Wolves: Contacting the Power of the Wild Woman (Classic Edition)) [By: Estes, Clarissa Pinkola] [Feb 2008].* Rider.

Haddish, T. (2019). *The Last Black Unicorn* (Reprint ed.). Gallery Books.

Li, M. P. S. (2021, December 31). *Importance of Play in Early Childhood (9 Benefits & Infographic)*. Parenting For Brain. https://www.parentingforbrain.com/benefits-play-learning-activities-early-childhood/

Pryor, K. (2020). *Don't Shoot the Dog! The New Art of Teaching and Training*. Lulu.com.

Robinson, L. (2021, December 9). *The Benefits of Play for Adults*. HelpGuide.Org. https://www.helpguide.org/articles/mental-health/benefits-of-play-for-adults.htmTedeschi, P., Jenkins, M. A., & Perry, B. D. (2019). *Transforming Trauma: Resilience and Healing Through Our Connections with Animals (New Directions in the Human-Animal Bond)*. Purdue University Press.

Recommended for Victuals

Afua, Q. (2001). *Heal Thyself: For Health and Longevity*. Eworld.

Ashby, M. (2005b). *Kemetic Diet: Food for Body, Mind and Spirit (Food for Body, Mind and Soul)*. Sema Institute.

Ehret, A. (2018). *Mucusless Diet Healing System*. Benedict Lust Pubs.

Henele, D. (2022). *Energetic Health: Interesting Insights Into Advanced Natural Medicine (Volume 1) by Dr Henele (2013–10–01)* (3rd ed., Vol. 1). CreateSpace Independent Publishing Platform; 3rd Edition edition (2013–10–01).

Mateljan, G. (2006). *The World's Healthiest Foods: Essential Guide for the Healthiest Way of Eating* (1st ed.). GMF Publishing.

McNish, D. (2012). *Eat Raw, Eat Well: 400 Raw, Vegan and Gluten-Free Recipes*. Robert Rose.

Moritz, A. (2012). *The Amazing Liver and Gallbladder Flush* (Updated Revised ed.). Ener-chi.com.

Robbins, J. (2012). *Diet for a New America: How Your Food Choices Affect Your Health, Happiness, and the Future of Life on Earth Second Edition* (25th Anniversary ed.). HJ Kramer/New World Library.

Wolfe, D. (2008). *The Sunfood Diet Success System*. North Atlantic Books.

Recommended for Exercise

Goggins, D. (2020). *Can't Hurt Me: Master Your Mind and Defy the Odds - Clean Edition.* Lioncrest Publishing.

Kaminoff, L., & Matthews, A. (2012). *Yoga Anatomy* (Second ed.). Human Kinetics.

Kapit, W., & Elson, L. M. (2013). *The Anatomy Coloring Book* (4th ed.). Pearson.

Long, R., & Macivor, C. (2006). *The Key Muscles of Yoga: Scientific Keys, Volume I* (3rd ed., Vol. 1). Bandha Yoga.

Mikkelsen K, Stojanovska L, Polenakovic M, Bosevski M, Apostolopoulos V, Exercise and Mental Health. Maturitas. 2017 Dec; 106:48-56. doi: 10.1016/j.maturitas.2017.09.003. Epub 2017 Sep 7. PMID: 29150166.

Recommended for Socialize

Ashby, M. (2017). *Guide to Kemetic Relationships: Ancient Egyptian Maat Wisdom of Relationships, a: Ancient Egyptian Maat Wisdom of Relationships, a Comprehensive . . . Peace, Progress and Spiritual Enlightenment.* Sema Institute.

Guy, L. (2021). *Overcoming Toxic Emotions: A Practical Guide to Building Better Relationships with Yourself and Others.* Skyhorse.

LCSW, L. S. M. (2013). *The Self-Esteem Workbook for Teens: Activities to Help You Build Confidence and Achieve Your Goals* (Illustrated ed.). Instant Help.

Leu, L. (2015). *NONVIOLENT COMMUNICATION: Companion Workbook - A Practical Guide for Individual, Group, or Classroom Study* (2nd ed.). Puddle Dancer Press.

PhD, B. K., & PhD, N. K. (2017). *The Self-Compassion Workbook for Teens: Mindfulness and Compassion Skills to Overcome Self-Criticism and Embrace Who You Are* (Illustrated ed.). Instant Help.

Participate in an Act of Selfless Service

- Purchase seven or more books, sign them below, and hand them out to random people. Keep one for yourself.
- Donate your copy of the book to a friend, family, neighbor, or random person.
- Buy an electronic version of this book to keep handy as a reference.
- Post on social media formats your experiences and #octavesmethod

You are giving a gift to help others heal their mind and find wellness, happiness, and success.

Made in the USA
Columbia, SC
18 October 2024